Who's Better Than Me?

A Guide to Living Happily Ever After

Nancy Witter

This book is dedicated to the love of my life,
"My Lovie," Jack Bella. Thanks to you,
I'm living happily ever after!

Contents

Introduction: Who's Better Than Me?   1

Chapter 1: You're Not Getting Older.   9
You're Just Getting Started!

Chapter 2: Mother Knows Best   25

Chapter 3: All Grown Up...Now What Do I Do?   43

Chapter 4: Behind Every Successful Woman Is   63
Herself

Chapter 5: We Will Never Be Who We Once Were.   85
We'll Be Better.

Chapter 6: I Love Myself, and This Time I Mean It   101

Chapter 7: Health Begets Happy   119

Chapter 8: It's Not Gray. It's Called Platinum!   131

Chapter 9: The Best is Yet To Come   151

Chapter 10: Good luck and God Bless!   171

Acknowledgments   189

About the Author   193

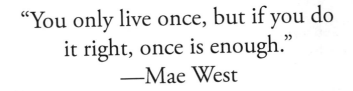

"You only live once, but if you do
it right, once is enough."
—Mae West

Introduction:

Who's Better Than Me?

Many years ago I was at a fundraiser in New York City that was packed with celebrities. As I looked around I saw Betty Buckley, Lena Horn, Alan King, and then I spotted Morley Safer from *60 Minutes*. I told the friend I was with that I was going to go say hi to him.

She was shocked. "You can't just go up and talk to him," she said. "Why would he want to talk to you? Nancy, please. You'll just humiliate yourself!"

"Look," I told her. "Just because he is more famous than me, makes more money than me, and is smarter and more successful than me, doesn't mean he is better than me."

"Actually, I think that is the definition of someone being better than you!"

I laughed, but when I saw he was free, I approached him. Courtesy of some Chardonnay, I said: "Morley Safer? Don't you recognize me? You're in my living room every Sunday night."

"I know young lady," he responded. "And you should put some clothes on!" Clearly, he had some wine too!

We had a wonderful lighthearted brief conversation. It gave me a fun brush with celebrity, and it taught me a great lesson. Whether it's Morley Safer, or anybody else for that matter, there will always be better and worse people than you, so what is the point of comparing? We will either feel unjustly confident, or unjustifiably insecure. It took some degree of confidence to boldly introduce myself to Mr. Safer. On my way home, I laughed and thought proudly and comically: "Who's better than me?"

Who's Better Than Me? is how I want every woman to feel about herself and her life. Life is hard enough, so we need every bit of confidence and self-respect we can muster. I don't care if you just parallel parked into a great spot, received your PhD in archeology, got 20 percent off a great pair of shoes, or just gave birth to triplets. After each one these events, large and small, you should roll your eyes upward and with a sly grin, say to yourself: "Who's better than me?" Even if you don't believe it at first, keep saying it over and over again and eventually you will. We need to lighten up on ourselves, find the humor in our shortcomings, take some chances, and know perfection isn't perfect. My imperfections taught me every valuable lesson I ever learned. My mistakes were my teachers; my humor and wit were my armor; and my family was my strength. We are all perfectly imperfect.

We need to learn how to love ourselves

unconditionally at any age, any weight, rich or poor, single or married. We have no problem loving our children, our parents, and our pets unconditionally, and yet when it comes to ourselves, we place the bar impossibly high. We look in the mirror and say:

"You're too old."

"You're too fat."

"You're an idiot."

Do you think you would ever speak like that to one of your friends? Of course not! You love your friends and see them through benevolent eyes. It is my hope that you will use the same eyes to see yourself. This book is about telling women the truth—that getting older is not only a blessing, but it can be as fun, as exciting, and as challenging as you want it to be. There is still so much to learn and explore. It gives us the freedom to do what we always wanted to do, after doing all the things we had to do. We have been set free from the old paradigm that life is worth less as you get older. Right now you are younger than you'll ever be, and yet, older than you've ever been. You know more than you've ever known, and you are better than you have ever been in almost every way. I prefer to think of it as playing on *Varsity*.

The degree to which you enjoy playing on Varsity has nothing to do with your athletic prowess, but everything to do with how you choose to see yourself and view your world. I want this book to be a manual of sorts. I'm sharing my story here, and I hope it will help you to disregard your fears, and ignore your perceived inadequacies—things we all feel from time to time.

In our lives, we have all seen heartache, tragedy, injustice, and inequality. We can't escape it, but we can battle it with intelligence, love, optimism, and humor. These are our weapons. That is what will protect us and help us through both the hardest, and the greatest, days of our lives. It is overcoming life's constant challenges that gives us our "life muscle." It makes us strong and resilient. By creating the life we love, we learn how to live happily ever after!

So ask yourself again: "Who's better than me?

The answer should always be:

"Absolutely no one."

"Mothers, food, love, career...
the four major guilt groups!"
—Cathy Guisewite

Chapter 1:

You're Not Getting Older. You're Just Getting Started!

Who is better than me? The answer should always be: absolutely no one! This is a fun yet powerful mindset. Learn it. Love it. Believe it.

But there's also another phrase I want you to say to yourself:

"You're not getting older.

You're just getting started!"

Once we accept and embrace who we are, we can move full speed ahead with our lives. With a more positive point of view, getting older can be absolutely empowering. Of course, aging is not without its OMG moments. But life wouldn't be any fun without those moments—most of the time.

I remember all too well that morning when I looked in the mirror and screamed. What was my mother doing in my mirror staring back at me? You probably have experienced this too, and I have to say: congratulations you are your mother's daughter, and you have finally become a middle-ager. It's kind of like being a teenager except you're older, wiser, and you don't have pimples...or a curfew!

On my fiftieth birthday, a dear friend said to me: "Welcome to the second half of your life. It's the best." This has proven to be true for me, and for most people I know over the big 5-0.

I enjoy my life in my fifties more than at any other time before. When you are younger there is a greater potential for screwing up, and the consequences can last a lifetime. I think (I hope!) I've made most of my major mistakes by now, and I've learned a lot from them. Now I feel brave enough to embrace success or risk failure. It was this kind of thinking that gave me the courage to say yes to my husband when he proposed to me just as I was turning 50, after being single for 20 years. I thought, if it doesn't work out, well, he's 60 and I'm 50. How much longer am I going to have to live it?

Since we're going to be spending some time together as you read this book, I thought I'd start by sharing my story.

Turning 50 was a defining moment for me. At first I felt relief—that so much of the hard work of living was behind me— and then a sense of excitement for what the future holds. At this stage I thought I'd better become whatever it is I want to become. My new mantra is: "If not now, when?" Writing a book has always been on bucket list, but now at 56, I feel like I finally have something worthwhile to write about.

When I did an inventory of what I have been through and accomplished and put it on paper, it felt impressive. It reminded me of a line George Constanza once said on *Seinfeld*: "You know if you take everything I've ever done in my entire life and condense it down into one day, it looks decent." So with that idea in mind, here are the highlights of my life condensed into a few pages.

I was born Nancy Jane McDougal the sixth of seven children of Walter and Dolores McDougal. My mother died when I was 15-years-old. My father remarried Phyllis O'Connor who had nine children, so I became the proud member of a family of 16. I did not attend college, but I did go to Alice B. Skinner Secretarial & Finishing School. Soon after I graduated I found a job at a firm called Communispond, which trained executives in public speaking. I worked during the day, and I took acting courses at night at the American Academy of Dramatic Arts.

At 23, I married Jimmy Witter, and we moved to San Antonio, Texas for nine months. When we returned, we found an apartment in Floral Park, New York, and I got a job at in the human resource department at Stone & Webster in Manhattan. In 1983 and 1984 my two children, Annie and Michael, were born less than a year apart. My Aunt Nancy, who helped raise me after my mother died, informed me that when children are born under a year apart they are referred to as Irish twins. I, however, refer to them as my financial vampires. My Michael was born on December 20th, and I came home with him on Annie's first birthday on December 22nd. I always referred to that week as my suicide week—two birthdays and Christmas within five days!

When the children were young, I worked several jobs, which included teaching defensive driving, becoming an exercise instructor at Lucile Roberts, and selling Nutrisystem programs. I separated from Jimmy Witter when I was 30-years-old, and in September 1987, I bought a co-op and signed my divorce papers on the same day. I found a full-time job at E.F. Hutton in Garden City, New York. After the crash of 1987, the company merged with Lehman Brothers, and within a week I secured a job at the newly formed Shearson Lehman Hutton. To keep that job, I was required to take and pass the Series 7 and 63 stockbrokers licensing test within a month. I hate math. It was my worst and weakest subject, but I passed it the first time out, a rare feat in 1987. To this day it stands as one of my proudest achievements. I worked in the brokerage industry for 10 years and banking for 13 years after that. That was as much of corporate America as I could stand.

I've also lived through some traumatic events, including the time I was violently attacked by a man in a ski mask in the middle of the night in my bedroom. Though I managed to fight him off, I rode an ambulance to the hospital to be treated for a concussion, 25 stitches in my head, and a badly bloodied and bruised body. But I still managed to attend a wedding a day later. This man had done enough damage. I wasn't going to let him take away the joy of seeing my dear friend Karen Erickson marry John Munkenback. I was happy and grateful I had the strength to celebrate their marriage. The man was never found, and I still sleep in the same bedroom to this day. I managed to chase him away that night. You know that saying: "you should see the other guy"? To this day, a bragging point for me is that it was his blood that was found on my window sill. It gave me some peace of mind over the years, because I knew I could take care of myself. It was a silver lining to a dark cloud.

After my divorce I dated a very nice man who helped me fix and enhance my humble co-op. His hard work made my apartment beautiful, it was like a small version of *Extreme Home Makeover*, accept without a sad sap story, cameras, and free flat screen TVs. But he was a very troubled man and fighting many demons, and so we didn't work out as a couple. I am very grateful for all he did to restore pride in my apartment, thereby elevating pride in myself and my life. He did a lot with his hammer, nails, brawn, and generous spirit. A few days after we broke up he committed suicide. As if that wasn't bad enough, another ex-boyfriend, who was a homicide detective, was the one who came to tell me the news. So now you know why I drink.

During those years I raised my Annie and Michael as a single mother. I worked at a French bank during the day, and I took a comedy class at night. I ended up performing stand-up comedy every Saturday night for 10 years at Don't Tell Mama, a popular cabaret in New York City. The bank fed my kids, and comedy fed my soul. During those years I won several comedy awards, and made wonderful lifelong friends.

I even made it to TV. The first time was as one of five finalists on Nick at Nite's *The*

Search for the Funniest Mom in America. I teamed up with two other finalists, Karen Morgan and Sherry Davey, and for five years we toured the country performing in theaters with the hit comedy trio "Mama's Night Out." The Lifetime channel cast my daughter Annie and me on a half-hour edition of *Mom's Cooking*, and a year later I was featured on a faux-Iron Chef competition on Dr. Oz's show. Who's the famous one now, Morley Safer?

I even had a brush with the movie industry when I was cast in a movie called *Stags.* My tiny role (less than a minute) even involved a simulated sex scene. By now I would hope you figured out it was a comedy! Having a funny little sex scene with a movie star like Mark Giordano was the highlight of my movie career. Comedy or not, I will take it any way I can get it!

I quit smoking in January of 2003 (I was a terrible smoker), and in November 2003 I completed the New York City Marathon in seven hours, speed walking instead of running. It was the same year P. Diddy ran. We didn't walk together, but I could tell that he wanted to.

The following year I walked a marathon and a half (a little over 39 miles in two days) for the American Cancer Society and raised over $12,000 in honor of my sister-in-law Adrienne McDougal and my friends Jean Mancuso, and Carol Manire who are all, thank God, survivors.

In 2006, I met and fell in love with Jack Bella. He is the love of my life and we married on February 17, 2007.

During the great recession in 2008 I was downsized from the bank, so I went back to school at NYU to get my profes-sional certification in life coaching.

I lost my mother at 15, my father when I was 45, my uterus at 48, and my gall bladder 54. I still perform comedy and I'm starting a new career and business. At 56 I'm writing this book, so you can see I'm gaining and losing all over the place.

If I asked you what you've been doing for the last 25 years, it might look similar to all of this, or it could be totally different. During my life, I've been irresponsible, immature, resilient, courageous, bold, and meek. My life has been filled with many mistakes, but few regrets. I've endured disappointment, fear, and disillusionment. I also have had an abundance of laughter, fun, encouragement, and love. Things have always had a way of turning around when I least expected it, but only after I took some chances. My crowning achievement to this day is that I survived, found the courage to find love again, and that my kids are more successful than I am.

The best way for me to minimize the things that overwhelmed me was to make comedy out of my catastrophes. It gave me power over the circumstances that befell me. The ability to laugh at myself and turn almost any disaster into a joke or a bit was how I coped. By simply finding the funny in my foibles, I was able to override fear, insecurity, and discouragement. Having the courage to laugh at my life launched me into a more joyful powerful place. If it wasn't for all my shortcomings I'd have no material at all. As you read about them, I hope in the end you'll just end up feeling great about yourself too.

Our struggles are different as we age. Our physical bodies may begin to wane, but our minds are wiser than at any other time in our lives. So keep saying, "you're not getting older; you're just getting started." It may sound like a lie at first, but keep saying it until you believe it. When Jerry Seinfeld was preparing to take a lie detector test, George Costanza said it best: "Just remember, Jerry. It's not a lie...if you believe it." So, believe!

EXERCISE #1

At the end of each chapter there will an exercise to help sort out your thinking. I would suggest you find a nice notebook and a great pen. For $9.95 you can have your own personal notebook with your name and even your own logo on it if you want. It can be made to order online at sites like VistaPrint. It's cheap and so cool.

These exercises are for you alone, not to be published or read by anyone other than yourself, unless you want to share them. It will be your "Getting to Know You" book. So get out your notebook and let's get started.

1) List off all your major events:
   • Achievements
   • Highlights
   • Tragedies

Basically, I want you to write down your life from cradle to five seconds ago.

EXERCISE #1 (con't)

It may surprise and impress you to review what you've survived and what you've achieved.

2) Now, make up a title for your life story, and then pick your own theme song that fits your life.

Choose a song that you love that lifts you up and transports you. It's a way of seeing your life so that you are the star, and the hero. (And you can even picture it on the big screen with Jennifer Lawrence playing you at 20.)

Be kind to yourself and be boastful when it calls for it. No one is going to read it. It is a gift from you to yourself. It could be at best inspirational and fun, and at the very least, helpful. You'll have an overview of your life complete with a soundtrack and a title.

Have fun looking at your life.

"Don't save anything for a
special occasion.
Being alive is a
special occasion!"
—Erma Bombeck

Chapter 2:

Mother Knows Best

Last week I was looking at some family photos and came across one of my grandmother. She had those old round wire rimmed glasses on, a hat that looked like she borrowed it from the queen, sensible ugly shoes, and a long coat with a corsage on it. She looked like she was 80, and I found out that in that photo she was only 53!

For women in the 21st century those days are long gone, and we are now a generation of women that not only look better, but we are also smarter, braver, and on more equal ground than at any other time in our history. We learned from the best—our mothers and grandmothers—but we are a unique generation of women, aging beautifully.

The other day I found myself jealous when I saw a slimmed down Paula Deen on the cover of *Prevention*. She is one of my role models over 60. I'm pretty sure if I asked her would she rather be 65 or 35, I'm sure she would choose 65. She garnered more success over 50 than under 40. OMG! When did I start buying *Prevention*

Role Models

All of my role models are now over 50:

- Helen Mirren
- Dame Judi Dench
- Kathy Bates
- Betty White
- Oprah Winfrey
- Diane Sawyer
- Joan Rivers
- Maggie Smith
- Barbara Walters.

Who are your role models?

instead of *Cosmopolitan*.

My mother was my favorite role model. She was smarter than she knew, and wiser than she got credit for. I still remember some of my mother's best sayings:

"Nothing looks good when you're tired."

"Show me your friends, and
I'll show you who you are."

"Nothing good happens after midnight!"

My mother died when I was 15 and as sad and tragic as it was, she left my brothers and sisters and me in the good hands and heart of her sister, my Aunt Nancy. Aunt Nancy worked full time at Lord & Taylor, and she would come down and visit us on one of her only two days off. Every Wednesday she made the trip over the Throgs Neck Bridge to make sure our house was clean, curtains were washed, floors were mopped, and the refrigerator was full. She taught me to drive, and helped me pick out my graduation dress and plan my wedding. She was my second mother, and it required effort, love, and sacrifice on her part. I was fortunate because she had the same mother as my mother had, and so all that wisdom she shared with me came from the same tributary source—my grandmother.

There are lessons of generosity that one generation of women passes along to the next. It is what makes women exceptionally nurturing and giving. We have to be sure, however, that we take as good care of ourselves as we do the people we love in our lives. It is not selfish. It is necessary.

I like to think of each of us as a human well, full of cold clean water, the sustenance of life. Everyone is always coming for water from you—your husband, the kids, your friends, your boss comes, until the one day that it's your turn to go to the well and it is bone dry. It's very easy for that well to not get replenished. When that happens, it leaves us feeling tired, sad, and inadequate. We need to find ways of rejuvenating ourselves and our spirit, and we can't always rely on others to help us out. By doing so we will always have plenty of "water" to share with those who come to us in want. Lean on your friends, take some time for yourself, and create boundaries that save you from yourself.

The other lesson my mother taught me was the gift of gratitude. My mother was one of seven and had the good fortune to have two brothers and four sisters. When I was a child playing with my sisters, my mother would say, "always remember: you're very lucky to have each other." I say that to my husband when we are having a particularly happy moment. I'll just look at him and say, "we're very lucky to have each other." I am grateful every day for my children, my brothers and sisters, my husband, and my friends. It makes me happy to know I have so much love at my disposal. It reminds me of a quote I saw shared on Facebook: "It isn't happy people that are grateful, it is grateful people that are happy."

The way my parents raised me became

the blueprint of my life. And I can tell you that if you were to try and build off this blueprint, you would get the Leaning Tower of Pisa! Neither one of them were perfect, and they were far from ideal role models. They were, however, fun, unique, and vivacious people, and what I learned from them has served me well.

My mother was a small woman—about five foot three—with beautiful blue eyes, a warm smile, and a perfectly heart-shaped face with a turned up nose. Her name was Dolores Gleason, but she was known as "LaLa" or "Lal." She had a million friends, and loved nothing more than a great party. It was watching my mother and her friends that made me love being around women so much. I saw how they helped and encouraged each other. Where one was weak, the others would make up the difference with their strength.

My mother was a terrible housekeeper, but she was a fabulous cook and hostess. She loved giving parties. Approximately an hour before any party, her friends Betty,

Millie, Mary, and Peggy would take over the house. They usually arrived minutes after my mother had a full and total meltdown. So it was not unusual for them to arrive at a house filled with chaos, confusion, and hysterical children. There were carpets in need of a vacuuming, and a kitchen in need of order. We would practically weep with joy that we were rescued from my mother's insanity. It was like the cavalry had arrived. My mother was then set free to get dressed and made-up. Just the thought of those wonderful generous loving women still warms my heart to this day. My mother was a very lucky woman to have such supportive, fun friends, and the parties were always so worth it.

Like most women she loved to shop, and adored a bargain, but longed for luxury. She would come home from her shopping expeditions at Klein's (one of the first discount store in its day) and feel so smart because she was able to buy 10 pairs of shoes for $5.00. They would have these crazy five-minute specials. They'd make the sales announcement and my mother would fly to get as many shoes as she could grab. They never fit anyone but she would say, "they were only 50 cents a pair. How can you lose? I would say, "You lose when they don't fit anyone and no one wears them." But then she would just say, "but they're only 50 cents. How can you lose?" and I would just give up.

Though she loved a great bargain, she did have one sticking point—the lack of a proper mink coat. She had a mink stole but that was not the same thing at all. In the late 60s, a mink was the symbol that you had arrived. She was embarrassed that all her friends had mink coats and all she had was a mink stole.

One Christmas my father went out and bought my mother the most beautiful mink coat with her name engraved on the inside. Now all of us gathered around the fireplace after we came back from our first Christmas midnight mass. As we began to open our gifts, I found myself more excited about what my mother was getting than what my presents would be. That was the Christmas

I celebrated as a true grown-up.

To truly surprise my mother my father gift wrapped this beautiful mink coat in a Klein's box. As my mother tore off the gift wrap off she saw her nemesis on the box: Klein's. Her adorable smile faded, as her high hopes of a proper mink were once again dashed. We all knew about the mink and we were even more excited than my father was. She finally opened the box and put on a phony smile, as she pulled out of the box what she believed was a mink stole. I watched her face as the coat slowly unfurled and she began to realize it wasn't a stole, but an entire coat. She was totally beside herself. She called everyone she could think of to share her good news, and that Christmas day she never took that mink off.

The pricelessness of my mother's mink coat was not in the mink, but in the giving and receiving of the mink. It is a memory that still tickles me 40 years later, and it is one of the best my brothers and sisters and I have of our parents. My father was thrilled to give my mother something he knew she would adore. He got a kick out of seeing her so happy, and that he was finally able to make her feel like a Rockefeller!

Several months later I woke up and was freezing. I walked down the hallway and found the window wide open. I then noticed something hanging out the window and when I looked I found it was my mother's beloved mink coat. I went in to talk to her and noticed that she seemed to be having a very rough re-entry after an apparently fun Saturday night. I leaned over the bed and asked her if she was all right. She looked up at me like a little girl. Her face was a combination of shame and regret.

She said "I got drunk by accident last night. Nancy promise me, whatever you do, you'll never drink gin. Always remember anything you can drink with gin you can drink with vodka. You want a gin and tonic have a vodka tonic, you want a gin gimlet, have a vodka gimlet, because gin will do you in."

Then I remembered why I came into the room so I asked her about the mink and why it was hanging outside the window and she said "I spilled a gin and tonic all over it, it reeks of gin." My mother never could hold her gin.

Well, it was a fortunate thing that my father gave her that mink that year because in August of 1972 my mother was diagnosed with inoperable esophageal cancer. She died four months later on December 5, 1972 at the tender age of 49, two weeks after she arrived home from a vacation to celebrate her 25th wedding anniversary. She left behind seven children: Steven 24, Carol 22, Walter 21, Ditta 19 Paul, 17, Nancy 15, and Peanut 13, and, of course, my heartbroken father.

I learned a lot at 15. I learned that life can be tragic, and funerals can be fun. I learned laughing at yourself is a great pain reliever, and I learned never to drink gin in a mink coat.

More importantly, I learned that being perfect has nothing to do with living perfectly. My mother went out of her way to make others feel happy and good about themselves. She didn't have a judgmental bone in her body. She could have written the quote by the late great Dr. Seuss: "Be who you are and say what you feel, because those who mind don't matter, and those who matter don't mind."

When I turned 16, I quickly learned that death is a part of life, and that memories are magic. They are what's kept my mother alive to me all these many years. In the beginning remembering my mother was like holding a painful pin cushion with the pins all standing up. It hurt to think about her knowing I could no longer see her, hear her, or hug her. Over time, it is as if the pins have receded into the cushion and now I had a nice soft ball, full of memories I could pick out and access any time I wanted. Like magic! The memories which had caused me pain, now gave me comfort and joy. I always think that when the people I love die, I have more people in high places.

We as humans are pure energy contained in a physical shell. The law of conservation of energy says energy can neither be created nor be destroyed, but it can be transformed into a different state. This has always given me great comfort. Friends have asked me over the years if I'd like to see a spiritual advisor who communicates with the dead. I have always said no, because it would be embarrassing. I know my family is too lazy to talk to me from the other side. My father would say, "Tell Nancy I'll talk to her when she gets here. Right now I'm busy being dead."

So on those occasions that you feel bad about getting older, remember many have been denied the privilege. If you could ask my mother if she would mind having a few wrinkles, a little arthritis, in exchange for seeing her grandchildren, I think she'd make the trade.

What I learned from my mother is to live like there's no tomorrow because there may not be one. Had my father put off giving her that mink for another year, we would have been denied seeing her so joyful in her last year in life. Try to do all the things you really want to do and see what you want to see. Life is meant to be enjoyed. It is the object of the game. Do it while you are physically able and emotionally well. You can live with the beautiful memories and photos well into your twilight years. I know that I'd rather die in debt than with regret. Getting older should not be paralyzing, but freeing. The greatest thing is to be in a position where you have nothing to lose, and we have less to lose each year we live. Ain't life grand?

"Life should not be a journey to the grave
  with the intention of arriving safely in a
pretty and well-preserved body, but rather
 to skid in broadside in a cloud of smoke,
thoroughly used up, totally worn out, and
loudly proclaiming 'Wow! What a Ride!'"
—Hunter S. Thompson

Dolores Gleason McDougal
February 2, 1923 - December 5, 1972

EXERCISE #2 (con't)

I want you to think about nothing but you, your life, and how you want to live. I hope you will get the sense that we are here for a very short time, although I know at times it seems like it's taking forever. You have control over most of it, and for those parts that you don't, you have control over your reactions.

Remember, this should be fun.

This is, after all, your life!

EXERCISE #2

Now I'd like for you to see your life from after you exit. This is a classic exercise, and for good reason. Sometimes we have trouble envisioning our future. So let's look at our life from the end.

1) It may sound morbid, but I want you to write your own obituary. What do you want it to say about you and your life?

2) What would you like your grandchildren to read about you? What do you want them to be proud of?

This is a great way to prioritize the important characteristics of your life. Do you want it to say you were a wonderful mother and wife, an outstanding church member, a great friend, kind to animals and children, a corporate magnate, an irrepressible spirit, or all of the above? It will tell you a lot about yourself. Then you can plot backwards to get to that obituary.

"It is never too late to be
what you might have been."
—George Eliot

Chapter 3:

All Grown Up...
...Now What Do I Do?

In 1930, the life expectancy of men was 59 years and 61 for women. By 2010, it had increased to 76 for men and 81 for women. Social security and pensions were originally meant to help people through the last few years of their life. Some never got their pension or social security because they didn't live that long. Today we are living in a world with endless possibilities at almost any age. You can go to school when you're 40, graduate at 44, and work a solid 25 years, before enjoying 10 or even more years of retirement. Knowledge and training are more accessible than ever before, so our options are wide open. If the average person retired now at 65 she would live an average of nearly 14 years outside the workforce. That is a long time just to golf or travel.

We all have an obligation to keep giving to the world the talents we have been given, with the energy we have been provided. This can take the form of volunteer work, starting your own business, or making an income from your hobbies. The possibilities are limited only by our own vision. How wonderful would it be in your later years, when your obligations have been fulfilled, to do what you always wanted? When raising a family of hungry growing children, with college on the horizon, most of us did what we needed to do, rather than what we wanted to do. We worked hard our entire lives, and now is the time to begin to reap the rewards. For some it may mean the end of one chapter or the beginning of the next. It could involve a career change or a divorce; it may be time to sell the family home, or even to buy a new boat.

I have heard women say:

"I'm too old to start that."

"Who would want to hire me at my age?"

"It's too late to change."

What kind of attitude is that? Why wouldn't they want you? Who wouldn't want someone with insight and years of experience? Would you rather have a 60-year-old surgeon, with 5,000 open heart surgeries under his bealt, operating on you, or a 30-year-old doctor who has done 12? Age isn't a liability, it's an asset. But you may have to change your point of view a little to realize what you've got. You must remain current and fully engaged with our world if you want to play in it. No one will hire you if you list your skill-set as: "Familar with the Wang, telexing, and Pitman shorthand." You may have to take a computer class, or learn new skills, but it will be worth it to get where you want to go.

Several years ago I was at a party having a lively conversation with a very smart, intelligent, remarkable woman named Tracy. She asked me if I could help her think through a dilemma. She was considering going to acupuncture school. I thought it was a brilliant idea, but she was hesitant because she felt, at age 58, it might be too late to get in the game. She told me she wouldn't finish training for three years. She would be almost 62 before she could even get her practice started. But I didn't buy that argument. I told her: "Regardless of what you do in those three years, you're still going to turn 62. So why not spend the time doing something that you love?"

Tracy also wondering how practical it was. Would there be enough time in this new career to earn back what she had invested in? It was a valid question, but any time we start a new endeavor, especially if it's something we're truly passionate about, we have to believe that the money will follow. It was certainly a risk, but she would have the rest of her life to earn it back.

I encouraged her to follow her heart, and she did it. She began her schooling and when when we last spoke, she was working on her practicum, working with her professors, performing acupuncture on patients. She called me in a panic one day, and said, "I feel like I'm slower than the younger students. Studying is a real challenge because I can't remember as well as I used to, and it takes me longer to complete my course work. The other students answer the questions from the professors faster than me." What she was describing was nothing but fear, self-doubt, and intimidation. It was probably true that she might have to study harder because her memory may not be as sharp as a 27-year-old's. So what? I reminded her that she wasn't doing open-heart surgery where time was of the essence. The other students were probably too scared and preoccupied with their own performance to care about hers. She just needed to remain calm and confident. She brought all of her life experience to the table for her future patients and her empathy and compassion. At age 60, she had spent a lot more time cultivating these talents, than she had at 30.

She graduated in May 2013 and I couldn't be more proud of her, and to have been a small part of that process. Her story was part of the inspiration for writing this book. She stands as a shining example and source of pride to her family, friends, and peers. Bravo Tracy!

We are not necessarily meant to be just one thing our entire life. I was a single mother, a secretary, a comedian, a life coach, and now I'm a writer and motivational speaker. I've evolved into what I am supposed to be. We can reinvent ourselves as we grow and change. No matter how great your life has been, who wants to stay the same for an entire lifetime? We have to grow or we stop being relevant. Life changes, if it didn't you could still work as a switchboard operator or an elevator attendant. The first step is to take time to explore what we are good at. What is it we can do now that we could not do before?

How can we take new chances, find new interests, and look to your future in an entirely different way?

When I look at people who have done that successfully the list is impressive. I named some of my role models in the previous chapter, but it's worth it to name a few more—people who started their careers later in life, or transformed themselves after doing other things. These people are such an inspiration, and the list could someday include you! Take a look:

• **Rodney Dangerfield** was a salesman that morphed into an actor and comedian. He did not really start until he was 42. He had performed in clubs when he was younger, but stopped to work as a salesman.

• **Laura Ingalls Wilder** became a columnist in her forties, but did not publish her first novel in the *Little House* series until her sixties.

- **Frank McCourt** published *Angela's Ashes* and won the Pulitzer Prize for when he was 66. It was his first book.

- **Grandma Moses** began her painting career in her seventies after abandoning a career in embroidery because of arthritis.

- **Colonel Sanders** began his KFC franchise in his sixties and was a late-in-life financial success.

- **Ronald Reagan** was an actor, union leader, and corporate spokesman. He wasn't elected Governor of California until he was 55. He was nearly 70 when he was elected US President, and remains the oldest man to have served the office.

Imagine if these people thought they were too old to contribute, or if they never changed their trajectory. Don't deny the world the things you can give and contribute. All of us have special talents, whether you're a great organizer, good with numbers, a fine writer, photographer, cook, artist, poet or singer. Everyone has gifts to share and the world needs what you have.

My gift was comedy, and I didn't really discover it until I was 40. I had tried stand-up in the 1980s a few times with some success and had a lot of fun doing it. However, the demands of being a single mother with a full-time job made it too hard to pursue. Then in 1996, as I was turning 40, I had an unsettled feeling that I was just surviving and not thriving. Every day I walked into the bank and felt a little dead inside. There was nothing there for me that I excelled at. When people asked me what I did at the bank I would say I just "showed up." My job gave me my much needed benefits, a decent paycheck, and free school supplies for the kids. I loved the people I worked with, and in the break room I would keep everyone laughing day in and day out. So for my 40th birthday gift, my best friend, Carol Manire, knowing me inside and out, enrolled me in a comedy class in New York City. It culminated with a performance on my birthday at Stand Up NY, a Manhattan comedy club. It was so much fun and I killed, if I do say so myself! I had the immediate and instinctive feeling that this was my destiny.

For the next 13 years, I worked at the bank by day, and performed stand-up comedy on the weekends. I worked at a place called Don't Tell Mama on 46th Street every Saturday night for 10 years in a show called "The Poole Party." It won a Bistro Award, and some MAC Awards (Manhattan Association of Cabarets and Clubs), and I garnered 4 MAC Awards for Outstanding Female Comedian.

Many times when I was on stage I was the oldest person in the room. That was somewhat unique. It worked to my advantage and I loved it. While all the other comics were talking about not getting laid, living with their parents, and eating kitty litter after getting high, I joked about work, paying my bills, troubles with the kids, Weight Watchers, and stories of my Irish "Cathaholic" family. I loved sharing my shortcomings and inadequacies with my new friends, my audience. Comedians, singers, and the most talented people in New York City became my extended family, and I had the most exciting fun of my life every Saturday night.

Many women I talk to tell me they feel defeated because they believe as they get older their options get more limited, as they feel they can't compete in an any arena with their younger counterparts. But there is no age restriction for discovering what you want to do, or become. You will know when you find that thing that is authentically yours. It will sing to you. Just don't be afraid when you hear the song.

The feeling of malaise could also be because we are looking at ourselves through the traditional lens of society. In our culture, a woman's looks are her stock and currency, while men are often measured by their wealth and success. It's funny how money never gets old. Aging can be particularly difficult for those women who relied on their youth and beauty throughout their lives. As we age, we lose out on that attention to younger women. As we get older it's important that we know our own value. We need to stand up for ourselves and our lives. Once we do, we will surely change the world. We're the only ones smart enough to do it. We have a wealth of experience and knowledge that we need to share with the new generation so they can be even better. They don't know everything, no matter what they think. They don't even know that speaking on the phone is faster, easier, and more efficient than texting and spelling badly. We have to help them.

I believe that we are chock full potential, and it is that unrealized potential that makes us feel unsatisfied and underappreciated. Our minds can get so full with our dreams and goals, but we can easily underestimate our capabilities and get mixed up with fear and self-doubt. Making a big change can be confusing and overwhelming. But I always remember a great quote by motivational speaker and author Denis Waitley: "It's not what you are that holds you back, it's what you think you are not." W.C. Fields had a funnier take on it: "It ain't what they call you, it's what you answer to." Remember that you get to define who you are and who you're going to become. Don't let anyone else tell you who you can and can't be.

If you still feel confused and unsure of which direction to take your life, an exercise I always like is make a pro and con list. Before I did my first comedy gig I thought a lot about the pros and cons.

Here's what my list looked like:

> ## Cons:
>
> • I will not be funny and embarrass myself.
>
> • People will be mad and disappointed in my performance because they wasted their time and money listening to me.
>
> • I will be sad and disappointed in my own failure.
>
> • It will be the end of my dream.

Cons (con't)

• I have no control of the outcome of my efforts.

• I'm scared of the unknown.

• People will talk behind my back and say I'm not funny.

Pro:

• I will feel brave for having tried.

• I will have a stage to perform on, have fun, and make people laugh.

• I will find my God-given talent.

• It will be exciting and cool.

• I will be unique, and creative, and have my own voice.

• I will create my own success, not at the bank, but on the stage on my own terms.

• I will be a star in my own world.

• I will be proud that I felt the fear and did it anyway.

I don't have to tell you that pros won over the cons. I set aside my fear and went for it. Notice the words I used: "I set aside my fear." I was still nervous and afraid, but I tried to put it away to do what I so desperately wanted to do.

During one of these early gigs, my sister Ditta was backstage with me, and right before I went out, she asked me, "aren't you ever afraid you might bomb?"

"It's like being a cardiac surgeon," I told her. "You know going into every operation that there is a chance the patient could die. But you have to go in expecting nothing but a positive outcome otherwise you'd never be able to operate." A doctor knows this is part of his profession and as long as he wins more than he loses he's a success. That's how I feel. I go on stage thinking my material is hilarious, and most of the time it is. When I have an off night, I am as shocked as the surgeon who loses a patient. Thank God failure isn't fatal in my profession. That's why I'm not a surgeon, and if I was wrong more than I was right,

I'd just go out and get a job as a weather-man. I would have lost so much if I had been afraid to fail, afraid to try, or afraid to go after my dream.

We are what we are. Someone who writes is a writer, someone who sings is a singer. She may not be a published author, and he may never become a recording art-ist, but they are still writers and singers just the same. When I first started out, I used to say, "I do stand-up," rather than, "I am a stand-up comedian," as if it wasn't really who I was, as if I hadn't earned it. But once I was on television and started getting paid and going on the road, I was finally able to acknowledge that, not only that I was a co-median, but that I had been one all along. I just had to figure it out.

What are you that you're not giving yourself credit for? What is that some-thing that people tell you that you are great at, but you take your hand and swipe it at them? "Oh that? That's nothing." Stop ig-noring them because it's not nothing. Start listening already! Are you a great researcher, an artist, a motivator, a master knitter, a skilled runner? You need to give credit to yourself for whatever gifts and talents you've been blessed with.

Please, please, allow yourself the pleasure of knowing you can contribute to the world in your own way. You can choose to take your gifts to the next level or not. You already are all grown up, but no one is too old to discover who they want to be. All you need is a deep desire and a little courage. So don't let your age hold you back. I didn't, and Grandma Moses sure didn't either.

EXERCISE #3

Just as you would never attempt to drive cross country without a map or a GPS, you cannot expect to move in your life without a plan and direction.

This is your personal GPS it includes **Goals, Plans and Steps**, which will lead you in the direction of your dreams.

1) What would you love to do or be? Simply be honest and describe what it is you want your life to look like. The more detailed the better.

If it helps, start by asking yourself some of these questions:

- What are your strong points?
- What are your skills and talents?
- How much money do you want to make?
- Where do you want to live?
- What have you always wanted to learn?
- Who do you want to be?

- What do you think you have to do to make these things possible?
- How do you want to feel?
- What is your worst case scenario?
- What are you afraid of?

After you make your list, think about the action steps necessary to reach your goal. It may involve research or networking, updating your resume, or further education. It could involve a loan, incorporating, or moving. Write it all down, including the pros and cons, and then a list of what comes first.

Write ideas for getting creating the life you envision for yourself, and write down how long you think it might take. A goal is merely a dream with a deadline. It is fun to really discover within yourself what you really want, what you're afraid of, and what you believe. The idea is that you get fully acquainted with who you are and what you want. Then make a plan to go get it. Giddy up!

"A woman without a man is like
a fish without a bicycle."
—Gloria Steinem

Chapter 4:

Behind Every Successful Woman Is Herself

Once we decide what we want to do, what we want to change, or what we want to become, then all we have to do is believe we can manifest it. We are the ones who must be our own heroes. I know many women who have felt defeated when they haven't gotten the support they hoped for from their husbands, friends or colleagues. The successful ones were the ones who stood behind the belief they had in themselves or their idea.

In my estimation the biggest mistake women make is underestimating how great

The Perfect "Lady Killer" Cocktail

- 2 parts Belief
- 2 parts Confidence
- 2 parts Positive Thinking
- 2 parts Courage
- 2 parts Perseverance

I've never been good in math, but in my world this adds up to success.

A glass with two parts vodka and two parts cranberry is great, too!

their talents are. Sometimes the problem is they can't visualize their potential or believe they can be what, in fact, they already are.

My sister is a fabulous decorator. She has a true talent. She is like Martha Stewart, except she's nice, and has a good personality. She never went to school to study design, but she worked for a builder, decorated his model homes, and they went on to win big awards.

Her home is her showplace for things she picks up at antique shops, or stores along the way. She always has her eye out for that very special piece that will be perfect somewhere in her home. Her house was built by the builder she worked for, and the first thing I noticed when I saw her new home was her front doors. They were not only beautiful, but totally different from the other front doors on the houses in the area. She said she saw these beautiful doors years ago at an antique store and fell in love with them. She bought them and knew one day she would use them as her front doors. She just didn't know when. Twelve years later, when she spoke with her builder about plans for her new home she showed him the doors, and said: "Build the house around this." It would never occur to me to do something like that. That's how her decorator's mind works.

When she quit her job working for the builder, I begged her to go into business for herself. She knows so much about tiles, granite, kitchen planning, facets, color, textures, and scale of furniture to room size—all the things that someone needs to know when they either renovate, build, or decorate a house. I'm an idiot when it comes to that stuff, and I'm not alone. I tried to impress upon her that what she knows is valuable to many people out there.

Many times I asked her what her plans were for her talent and she would say: "I'm not a decorator. Nancy, just having nice taste doesn't make you a decorator, and I can't charge people when I'm not qualified." To help her feel more confident and authentic I suggested she might want to take a professional certification course in interior decoration. She worked for a builder and with clients for over 12 years and still did not know her value. I thought no one looked at Picasso and said, "I love it, but I'm not sure if he's an artist. Where did he get his degree from?" I encouraged my sister to take pictures and create a portfolio so people could see her work and judge for themselves whether they, as the client, share the same aesthetic.

She was still unable to see the potential that I saw so clearly. So I created a business card for her. I named it after a combination of her last name, Shupe, and her nickname, Peanut. (Her real name is Maryann but she has been called Peanut ever since that five pound baby girl came home from the hospital and 55 years later, I can't imagine calling her anything else.) I named her business:

Everything for your decorating needs... from *Shupe to Nuts!*

I even created a simple website that matched the cards. All she had to do was upload some pictures, and voilà. Sometimes you have to see it to believe it."

I wanted her to see her potential in a tangible physical way. She needed to work into it, define it, believe it, and achieve it. But this was her journey not mine. This was as far as I could take it. She never uploaded the pictures or did anything with the cards. She just wasn't ready to launch herself. Peanut was the one that needed to realize the magic in herself, and that goes for all of us. People can tell us we're beautiful, talented, smart, and unless, and until, we believe it ourselves, it is of no use to us. Think of Dorothy in *The Wizard of Oz*. She had the power to go home the entire time she was in Oz. It wasn't until she knew herself that she had the power that she could get herself home. Otherwise Dorothy would still be hanging out with munchkins, wizards, and witches.

For many of us, what we want, or wish we had, can seem so far out of our reach we just give up. That's why it is so important to be committed to our dreams and goals. If we're committed we will not let anything get in our way, not our circumstances, unsupportive people, or any other obstacles. Many times our fear is disguised as an obstacle, and we use it as our out. Now is the perfect time to overcome your fear and take chances. Be cognizant that at this point it is your belief system that leads you around. You either believe you can get what you want, or you don't. That is the true master of all of us. If you can picture it, your brain can believe it. As Buddha said: "All that we are is the result of what we have thought."

In high school I was the funny friend, and the terrible student. After my mother died there was no one at home to look at my grades, and my father wasn't interested in my scholastic activities. He didn't believe in women getting a higher education, even though he was a lawyer and a bank president. He thought it was a waste of money because he assumed we would all just get married, get what he called our "M.R.S." degree.

The only subjects I excelled in were drama and English. I could write stories and I could act. My father was a very funny and talented man himself. He boasted for as long as I could remember: "Nancy is going to go to drama school." So in the summer of 1975 I auditioned for the American

Academy of Dramatic Arts in New York City. I studied and memorized a monologue from *The Prisoner of Second Avenue* by Neil Simon. Even though I could never remember the date of the War of 1812, I could memorize any script. In the audition waiting room I was surrounded by people from Houston, Tampa, New Orleans, Colorado, Chicago, and others from all over the United States. It was a very competitive school to get in to, and I was sure they'd never pick me, but they did. Though I was never even in a school play, I was able to wow them at the audition and won a place in the fall class in 1975.

When I got home I called everybody I knew to tell them the great news. I was so relieved that I had somewhere to go in September. I was going to the American Academy of Dramatic Arts! My father was very proud and my future was set.

Well, it was set until the end of the August. I remember this moment so well, just like people remember where they were when JFK died or on 9/11. My father was getting ready to go to a black-tie affair. I walked into the bedroom, and I asked him for a check that was due for my tuition payment for the first semester. While he was fixing his tie in the mirror, he said in a very casual voice, "Oh I thought about it, and decided you're not going to go to The American Academy. I spoke to some of the guys at "The Club" and they were telling me it is really just a bunch of kooks that go to a school like that. I decided it would be best for you to go to secretarial school. If you know how to type you will always have a job. Just look at my secretary Marion Kranz. She has been with the bank for 27 years. She is going to get a nice pension, she has a great medical plan, and a 401K. That is a much better plan than a nutty drama school." Then he left to go to his dinner.

There was nothing in me but complete devastation. The thought that my father could decide my entire future based on nothing more than a casual random conversation with some acquaintance at "The

Club" was beyond my comprehension. Worse, was that he wanted me to be Marion Kranz. Marion was a true spinster who lived with her mother and a cat. She wore a lapel pin that she received for working at the bank for 25 years. That was her favorite piece of jewelry. Kill me!

Immediately I called and told my sister Carol. She was pregnant with her first baby which would be the first grandchild in our family. She talked me into coming out to North Dakota to help with the baby, and come up with a Plan B (it meant something different in 1975). Now you know your life is on the precipice of disaster when moving to Bismarck, North Dakota is your best option. It wasn't a great plan but it was a plan, and I knew if anyone could help me my sister Carol could. She was more like a mother to me than a sister.

I have always been grateful to her for giving me a soft place to land and for letting me come to figure things out. She provided me with love, attention, guidance, and support my entire life. Though I was the first, over the years "Camp Carol," as we call it, has been the place everyone in my family goes when they feel lost and have to sort things out. I adore her.

Carol is a college professor, and unlike my father, she thinks education is the most important thing in the world. She encouraged me to take some classes at the local college. I took a class in typing (of course) and psychology, and took care of my adorable nephew Casey during the day. In December I returned home. With a broken spirit and having lost all my confidence, I eventually thought it best to agree with my father and become a professional secretary. So in January of 1976, I became a full-time student at the Alice B. Skinner Secretarial and Finishing School.

The fact that my father wanted me to be "like Marion Kranz" had a lot to do with his outlook on life. He felt that I should have a practical alternative in case I never met my Prince Charming. He thought, as many in his generation did, that every woman needed to know how to type. It was a skill that would always offer financial security.

Looking back, it was probably an easy out for me. I thought, "I'm no one special. What was I thinking? Thank God Daddy saved me from myself and stupid dreams." With that belief system I never would have made it in show business. Unfortunately, my father's lack of support for my decision to go to acting school did a lot of damage to self-esteem. In my head and heart, I believed he tried to save me from the failure he knew I was destined to be. So without even failing, I felt like a failure just the same.

Though I finished school, I never did get a degree from the now defunct Alice B. Skinner Secretarial and Finishing School. It was my way of being a bit of a rebel. It made my father insane that I wouldn't finish my accounting credit to get that degree. Without a formal degree, I managed to get my first job in January 1978 at a company called Communispond in New York City. It was a company that taught executives presentation and public speaking skills, and I loved it.

After I saved enough money, I auditioned again for the American Academy of Dramatic Arts and, again, I was accepted. I attended night classes there for two years and paid for it myself. As motivational speaker and pastor Dr. Robert H. Schuller once said: "God's delays are not God's denials."

In the end I was a secretary for 20 years, but also an award-winning comedian. I managed to do what my father wanted me to do, and much later in life, to do what I wanted to do too!

It is important to be responsible for our own choices, and our own happiness. It wasn't up to my father to believe in me, it was up to me to believe in me, just as it is up to my sister Peanut to believe in herself. Over the years I have come to know if you really want to do something, nothing can stop you, and if you don't, nothing can make you. I wasn't ready to believe in myself back then in 1975. I could have fought for my own bright future, but in the depths of my soul I didn't believe I could do it, and I was too scared to try.

My life changed when I found the power of saying yes to everything—every job large or small. When I started doing comedy I even performed in a shoe store once.

Back when I first dipped my big toe in the pool of stand-up comedy my dear friend Cathy Demers moved from New York to Chicago. I got a call from her at 2:00AM on a Sunday morning. She told me she met a man who owned a comedy club in Chicago called The Funny Firm. She talked him into allowing me to perform in a guest spot when I came to visit her two weeks later.

"I told him you were on *Saturday Night Live*, and at Caroline's," Cathy said, "so all you have to do is call him. He'll interview you over the phone and book you."

I was scared to death, and I told her. "Cathy, I've only done three shows in my entire life."

But Cathy was smart. She said, "this is

your big opportunity. You're hilarious and they'll love you." I called the guy and lied my ass off. He believed me which means I am an outstanding bullshitter. I was booked, and off I went.

My friend Ron, a radio personality, gave me some priceless advice. He told me because I was from New York the audience might be a little hostile. He said to make a crack about how much better Chicago is than New York to put them at ease. I kept that in mind as I studied my set list on the plane.   I felt so brave on the plane. I thought, "I bet I'm the only one on this plane doing stand-up tonight."

Cathy picked me up at the airport, and when I got the club I was shocked. There was a line around block. The tech director introduced himself to me and asked about lighting. I had no idea what he was talking about. He asked what kind of light I want-ed him to flash to let me know my time was up. I didn't know what he meant, so I said: "I'll take a Coors Light." He thought I was kidding and laughed. By then I understood what he meant and picked the flashlight.

Cathy brought an entourage of about 15 people from work. As I was getting ready for my introduction, I was scared out of my mind. The place was packed and I was an amateur. I couldn't even remember my name. I met a man named Bill in the wings where I was to stay until they called me on stage. He said he was at the club every night and not for me to worry. He said he would buy me a drink after my big debut. That calmed me down and then I heard my introduction.

"And now from New York City we have a comedian that has played on *Saturday Night Live*, David Letterman, and clubs all over the city...Nancy Witter!" The place went nuts and I was paralyzed with fear and hysteria. In that moment I thought: "It isn't what you know, or who you know, it's what they believe you know. They believe you're funny right now because this guy just told them you were. All you have to do is not be, well, not funny."

I took the stage and with all the energy

and excitement I could muster I said: "Hi everybody! I'm Nancy Witter and I just flew in from New York about two hours ago and I'm having a ball. I just can't figure out why they call this the Second City. I'm never going home."

They loved it and for the next six minutes I had them laughing and applauding. I got off the stage and Bill was ecstatic. He whisked me off in his Lamborghini to a fancy place around the corner to celebrate. We were there for about an hour, and then he took me back to the club just as people were filing out.

He opened the door and there was my clueless friend, Cathy. She had been panicked and screamed at me: "Where have you been? I came to see you after your set, and the guy there told me you left with someone. I told him that was impossible that you didn't know anybody, and now here you are with this guy in a Lamborghini?"

And you know what I said: "Who is better than me?"

People asked me for my autograph and

later that night the owner called to say he had heard great things about me. He asked if I would like to perform again the following night. I'm not stupid and I was not at all sure that I could duplicate that success again, so I told him I was booked somewhere else. It still remains as one of the most exciting, thrilling, exhilarating nights of my entire life. The lesson I learned was to say yes, take chances, and believe you can do it.

The litmus test to see how much you want to pursue something, is to see what you would give up to get it. If the answer is nothing, then it is not the right thing to pursue. My life could have gone in many directions but no matter what, I think I would have landed in the same place. Even if I could, I would not go back and change a thing. I never would have learned the lessons I learned along the way. Everything important I ever learned came after a mistake. But it's helped me build the story of who I am today.

We all tell ourselves a story of our lives that we absolutely believe. Every experience we have requires us to process it in our minds. How we process this becomes our story. Let me give you an example. Suppose you date a man who you are incompatible with. He is selfish and unkind and he ends up breaking up with you. Then let us suppose the story you tell yourself about that experience is: "I'm unloveable."

When your next love affair comes along you may bring that same story with you. More often than not, it becomes a self-fulfilling prophecy. Should the love affair fail, you will once again tell yourself the story that you are "unloveable," even though it's not true.

If you've had very few successes in your life you may tell yourself: "I've never succeeded at anything. I'm a loser." Once you start to believe these negative stories, unbeknownst to you they come to fruition. These stories and accompanying feelings are simply your interpretation of the experience, and an interpretation can be changed.

Reflect and try to discover what you really believe about yourself because it is what is ruling your life. Start by writing. We may not always know what is going on in our subconscious minds, but once we begin to write it pours out. Writing is a way to access those inner thoughts and beliefs. What you believe controls your thoughts, your feelings and your actions. A positive interpretation of your life will take you a lot farther than a negative one any day. If you can change what you believe about yourself, anything will be possible.

EXERCISE #4

Let's examine what you believe about yourself and why—the good and the bad. Perhaps you can tell yourself a new and improved story. In this exercise, I want you to write some letters. You're not going to send them to anyone, so be honest and thoughtful about your feelings.

1) Write a letter to someone in your present or past, dead or alive who has encouraged and believed in you. Thank them and write how it influenced and changed your life.

2) Now write a letter to someone who did not support you and compromised your belief in yourself. Write how it affected your confidence, and the story you've been telling yourself about it.

3) Lastly, I want you to write a third letter to yourself. Remind yourself of one thing you wanted to do but didn't because you didn't believe you could. And then tell the story of something you did do even though you might have been afraid, and had a great outcome. Sometimes we need to remember how great we can be, and who better to tell us than ourselves?

"To improve is to change;
to be perfect is to change often."
—Winston Churchill

Chapter 5:

We Will Never Be Who We Once Were. We'll Be Better.

We will go through many transitions as we pass age 50, 60 and beyond. We will have to face some of our fears about the changes we will encounter be they situational, emotional or physical. Once we find the courage and fortitude to accept these changes, and adopt an optimistic attitude about them, the happier we will be. Self-acceptance is the greatest gift we can give ourselves. Years ago I can remember the disdain I felt for my body, which was much better then, than it is today. Today, I just can't find enough energy for all the self-loathing that I used to have. I try to stay in shape and be healthy, but unfortunately fun, friends, dinners out, and great wine often prevent my best intentions. By the way, you look better now than you will 15 years from now. Don't believe me? Go find a picture of yourself taken 15 years ago. Most of us will say, "I thought I was so fat back then. How did I not know how fabulous I looked?" With that knowledge in mind, I simply accept, as Popeye used to say: "I am what I am!" Snooki would have no idea who Popeye is, but I know you guys do.

Who wants to read a memoir by Snooki or Miley Cyrus or Kim Kardashian? What can they tell any of us? The women I am rooting for and the women I want to read about are the ones who have raised families with their mate or on their own; the ones that have gone to work and have had successful long-term careers; the ones who have taken a chance and the ones who failed, but tried again; and the brave women who left bad marriages, as well as the ones who survived heartbreaking widowhood. I want to

know more about the women who have survived breast cancer, heart attacks, and other
health crisis and press on.

We, as a collected group, have so much
to offer the world. We are also the spoil-
ers, as we tend to be our own worst enemy.
Our limits are only those that we impose
on ourselves. I notice now that the older I
get, the older my definition of "old" is. As
Victor Hugo once said: "Forty is the old age
of youth; fifty is the youth of old age." So
I guess I am, once again, youthful. Humor,
self-acceptance, and a positive point of view
will make us the Golden Girls of this generation. Who's better than us?

The trick is to accept and come to
terms with the changes and transitions we
encounter as our life changes. I've made
some major transitions in my life and with
it came confusion, angst, and resistance
which is part of the process of transitioning.
That is how change is—it's scary and uncomfortable. Acceptance is the key, and it
brings with it peace, which is the by-prod-
uct of change. Often we experience a feel-

ing of loss, as is expected any time we grow. We give up some things, to make room for other things. A flower has to push away the dirt to come up out of the ground, to leave the safety of the cool, dark underground to be able to bloom in the brightness of the sun. I never thought flowers were brave, but they are. Sometimes, to give ourselves a better life, we need to be as brave as flowers.

For me, to have a better happier life I knew I would had to be brave enough to divorce my first husband. I was divorced when I was 30 and was a single mother for 20 years. Divorce is now becoming more frequent for those over 50. Some sources say that the rate for divorce in that age bracket has doubled over the last 20 years, and I think there are several reasons for the rise.

We are a generation that grew up in era where divorce became more socially acceptable. We are also living longer and with a better quality of life. You could divorce at 55 and still live another 30 years. Who wants to waste those 30 years with someone who doesn't make you happy. Women are also more independent than ever before. Many of us have had careers and are financially and emotionally capable of taking care of ourselves. So things are different than they were for our parents and grandparents. That being said, it doesn't mean that divorce is easy. It is rife with fear and anxiety, and requires a great deal of fortitude. Feelings are hurt, children are upset, money and possessions are fought over, and rarely does anyone think their share is fair. It is though, the price of freedom and for many the only path to find peace and happiness.

When I got divorced I totally lost my mind. I had initiated it, and had two small children under the age of three to take care of. My marriage ended because I couldn't be who he wanted me to be, and he was not who I needed him to be. While I was home with the children, he was either at work, school, rugby games, rugby practice, tending bar, and being a bouncer at a local tavern. He was never home and I was lonely and felt emotionally neglected. Never had I felt less loved and more devastated in my life. If I stayed I knew a part of me would die, and I wasn't willing to let any part of me die. I was not willing to make that kind of sacrifice and to live, what I knew would be, an unhappy and ultimately unfair life for all involved. What I had to do would be the most difficult thing I ever did. I ended my marriage.

At the end, just before he walked out the door, he looked at me and said: "What do you think you are going to do without me?" I said defiantly with a false sense of bravado "Don't worry about me. I'm going to be just fine!" I slammed the door and then smiled with self-satisfaction. This didn't last long, as I slid down to the floor and thought: "Oh for the love of God! What am I going to do?" Here I was a woman with a high school diploma, a mortgage, and two kids looking at me like baby birds waiting to be fed the worm and no job.

Regardless of my less than perfect circumstances, divorce was the right thing to do. I knew it, I acted on it, and I never regretted it. When you are fighting for your life, you find strength you never knew you had. Forgiveness is what helped me the most. I found a way to forgive my ex-husband Jimmy, but more importantly, I had to forgive myself.

Looking back I think I felt guilty because I was the one that changed so much during our marriage. My mistakes and missteps impacted the implosion of this marriage. I played a little drinking game back then, it was called "feel a feeling, do a shot!" I was running around the fire instead of walking through it. I was avoiding pain, and by doing so, causing more. I surrounded myself with chaos, friends, comedy, beer, cigarettes, music, and more false bravado. I was irresponsible and reckless, and though a loving mother, I was not always present. I saw how messy and scary life can get. Many times I felt like a coward, and had no idea how to heal. Finally, I found my way into therapy and it changed everything. "Saint Irene," my therapist, worked with me for seven long painful and insightful years. She was the hero I needed.

Healing begins when we are brave enough to breakdown, so we can build back up. You have to find the strength to recover from the rubble, rebuild your soul, and redirect your life. Looking ahead with hope, instead of behind with regret. My heart had in its core, a special love for Jimmy. It occurred to me that I couldn't love my children, without loving their father. We were the only two people in the world that were the parents of Annie and Michael, and no one could love those kids quite the way we did. If I were to have a happy future I knew I had to find a way to leave him, but still love who he was.

This forgiveness thing has made us a happier family. We live in different houses with different spouses, but we are a family just the same. I always kept the future in my vision. I knew there would be weddings, christenings, and grandchildren's birthday parties in our futures. We had to find a way to stay on good terms even when sticky issues conspired to keep us fighting. One of us had to roll our eyes and give in for the greater good. Sometimes he did, and sometimes I did. The kids were grown and gone before we knew it, and college graduations and other big celebrations were more joyful because we weathered the storm. It was not easy, not always pleasant, but it served us very well in the long run. I barely remember what we ever fought about. Today Jimmy and my new husband Jack are very good friends. We have we come a long way in 25 years!

If you should find yourself going through a divorce, lean on your friends, see a therapist, cry, feel the pain, and hold your ground. If you have a friend going through a divorce, be patient, and non-judgmental and let them be "Nutty McGee" for awhile. They'll make mistakes, and have some regrets, but it is a process that unfortunately can't be skipped over. They'll lose their minds for a bit, but give it a minute, and they'll be back. Be generous with your heart, have big ears, warm hugs, and lots of wine and tissues.

We've talked a little bit about this already, but the other major obstacle we encounter when in any transition is fear. It is the glue that keeps us stuck. It is the voice that says, "you can't do this." The first thing you need to do is recognize the voice of fear. Then you need to tell it to shut up. The insidious thing about fear is that it comes in many forms. There is fear of failure, fear of success, fear of loss, fear of appearing foolish, fear of rejection, fear of losing, fear of embarrassment, fear of facing the truth, and I could go on and on. But we've got to learn to let it all go.

Once we accept who we are, and forget about what other people think, the more powerful we feel and the less of a grip fear will have on our psyche. My mother used to say to me: "It's none of your business what people are saying behind your back," and she was absolutely right. It is something we have no control over. When you fear you're not good enough in some way, or that people are judging you, or your clothes, or your weight, or your lifestyle, then suddenly you're a hostage to how you appear to others. You stop being who are and begin being what you believe other people want you to be. That is where we begin to lose ourselves.

Some fears are more difficult than others to let go of, but now is the time to discover your courage and to live boldly. Aren't we old enough not to care? I mean when you're a teenager you almost can't help it. When you're young you want your peers to be impressed with your life. But now, what's holding you back? Who cares what anyone else thinks? Don't let anyone else's opinion of you—or even your perception of their opinions of you—stop you from doing the things you want to do, being the person you want to be, and living that platinum life.

Barbara Walters once asked Katherine Hepburn to describe herself, and she said she was like a mighty oak. Maybe you're not a world famous actress with four Oscars, but who says you can't be a mighty oak too? We should only fear not taking enough chances and regretting the things we didn't do.

Surround yourself with like-minded people, people who will build you up and help you live fearlessly. Go boldly into the future with wishful thinking coupled with meaningful actions, and an optimistic attitude that your future is going to be brighter than it ever was before.

I love musicals, and music has gotten me through many tough times. There is a song I used to listen to whenever I needed to feel brave. It was from *The King and I*. Mrs. Anna played by Deborah Kerr is afraid as she and her young son arrive in Siam. She sings a song to him to calm his fears. It is a little bit like "fake it until you make it," but I always loved it and sing it to myself whenever I feel fearful. Part of the lyrics are:

"Whenever I feel afraid, I hold my head erect and whistle a happy tune, and no one will suspect I'm afraid. While shivering in my shoes, I strike a careless pose, and no one ever knows I'm afraid. The result of this deception is very strange to tell. For when I fool the people I fear, I fool myself as well. Make believe you're brave, and the trick will take you far, you may be as brave as you make believe you are!"

Aren't they beautiful lyrics? Thank you, Rogers and Hammerstein.

Living fearlessly is when you don't care if you try and fail, or look foolish, or care what people might think if you leave the country club, sell your house, go back to work, or put on a few pounds, only then will you know real freedom! The author Joyce Meyer once said: "Do it afraid." Sometimes that's the answer. Be who you are, make no apologies and work with fear not against it.

We are a brave bunch. We can battle divorce, combat fear, and come out victorious! Who's better than us? I was never this brave at 30. Every day we get older, wiser, and braver. There nothing we can't do once we love and accept ourselves. It gives us great strength, so strike a careless pose and be as brave as you make believe you are!

EXERCISE #5

1) Imagine if you could do anything without fear and no risk. What would it be? How would it feel? Describe this situation in as much detail as you can.

2) Then write down a list of what's holding you back, and what you're fearful off. Look at the list and think about how easily it could be to just let go of those things.

3) What would you let go of? What would happen if you let go of it?

4) What do you want to do, but are too afraid? Which steps would you have to take to do it? Write them down, and then try out step one. Maybe it's not as scary as you thought. Before you know it, you may have accomplished one of your goals.

"I'm good enough, I'm smart enough, and darn it people like me."
—Stuart Smalley

Chapter 6:

I Love Myself...
And This Time
I Mean It

The longest monogamous relationship you'll ever have is with yourself. You can't break-up with yourself, so you have to learn to love yourself. I've been to workshops and lectures, and read hundreds of self-help books. One theme they all seem to agree on is the importance of affirmations. An affirmation is often thought to be an exercise where you look in the mirror and say ridiculously wonderful things about yourself whether you believe them or not. We've talked about affirmations in other chapters, in a slightly less direct way.

The concept is great because it's a way

to get those positive thoughts to seep into your subconscious and to start to change your beliefs about yourself. So if we write, speak, feel, and hear all these wonderful things about ourselves, we will reap the greatest rewards for ourselves. It fosters self-love and acceptance and most beneficial it gets directed to our subconscious.

The problem is, most of us can't look in the mirror and with any level of sincerity say: "I love you, you are a gorgeous, smart, wonderful woman." It brings back memories of those *SNL* skits with (now Senator) Al Franken as Stuart Smalley: "I'm good enough, I'm smart enough, and doggone it, people like me." I've tried it and not only do I not believe it, but I feel like a complete jackass in the process.

So my suggestion is to start simple. Go with something you can say and believe. I never thought I was pretty, smart, thin, or successful, and I know I wasn't rich, I'm also smart enough to know when I'm kidding myself. At 56, I do think I'm beautiful. Beauty is more than "pretty," and more powerful than gorgeous. It encompasses the whole of a woman, which includes her spirit, heart, generosity, and her entire being. Pretty and gorgeous are adjectives usually reserved for young women—those of us that are not fully cooked yet. They are often terms used by people who can only see physical attractiveness in one dimension. I saw a beautiful elderly woman and a friend of mine said, "she must have been gorgeous when she was younger." I said, "she was probably very gorgeous, but she has developed and grown into the true beauty she is today."

When I look in the mirror, the affirmation, I sincerely say is: "You are kind, generous, insightful, and funny. People can benefit from the talents you have been blessed with. Go out and be the best you can be, the world needs it."

Your truth is surely different. You might say: "I'm beautiful and a hard worker, I am understanding and smart, and I'm proud of who I am." There is no blanket affirmation, but they only work when they are mixed with genuine feelings. In other words, just saying these words has little or no effect. It is the feelings that create the vibrational energy to bring these words and beliefs to life.

When we truly believe something about ourselves, we feel it. We feel confident, but not just because we say the words. It's because we know we're smart, or because we know we are talented. We believe it and we feel it.

Another effective tool is to say the things you want in your life, as if they are already present. For instance don't say, "I hope one day to be a fashion designer." Instead say, "I am a fashion designer." Remember a singer is a singer whether they have a signed recording contract or not.

When setting goals don't say, "I want to be 30 pounds lighter by the end of the year." Instead tell yourself, "I will be 30 pounds lighter in 2013." Then try to conjure up how that feels. It is the feeling that will get you where you want to go. It is removing all doubt from your mind. These exercises are very important because they not only reinforce positive feelings about yourself, but they also keep you focused on what you want to achieve.

So right now, put the book down and go look in the mirror. What do you want to tell yourself right now? Start with a simple affirmation and an easy goal to get yourself started. Once you get more used to it, you will build to bigger ideas and more important goals. When you're done, pick the book back up again because we're not finished yet!

You may have heard of this next technique. Athletes have known to use visualization before playing a big game to imagine a win. It is to see in your mind's eye that which you would like to manifest in your life. When I was starting out doing comedy I would practice my routines in the mirror, and I would visualize the audience laughing. I would imagine taking a bow, smiling, and how much fun it would be. It happened almost exactly as I envisioned it every time. We really can achieve whatever we put our minds to.

In order for your visualizations to be most effective, you need to really imagine your outcome in great detail, and do it often. At one time in your life you might have called it daydreaming. Well, that is exactly what it is. If we believe we are more competent, and have the power to manifest what we want in our lives, then our outcome is bound to be more successful.

The more you see the abundance in your life, and feel gratitude, the greater your perception is of your personal success. On the other hand, if you look at your life and just see what isn't there, that too becomes your reality. You think to yourself, "I didn't get the promotion; someone else got the big house we wanted; I'm not thin enough; I don't have enough money in the bank." These become the things you focus on. These negative thoughts will reinforce to you and in your subconscious mind that you don't have the power to attain the things in life you want. Your words and thoughts are your power, and they can either help you or hurt you. We can either become a casualty of our negative thoughts, or the beneficiary of our most positive thoughts. It's your choice. I'm reminded of this great quote:

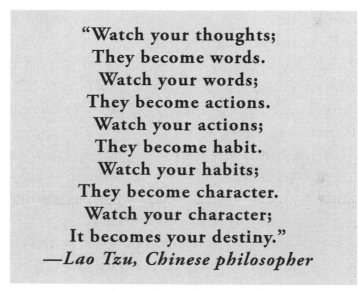

> "Watch your thoughts;
> They become words.
> Watch your words;
> They become actions.
> Watch your actions;
> They become habit.
> Watch your habits;
> They become character.
> Watch your character;
> It becomes your destiny."
> —*Lao Tzu, Chinese philosopher*

We need to think, plot, and believe we can achieve the things we want. Effort is the answer. Life requires effort. There may be resistance: your husband might think you're crazy; your kids might resent the fact that you are spending time and money on your pursuits rather than theirs—but this is your life, and it's important. It's worth the effort!   When you help yourself you help all those connected to you.

After you help yourself, the effort spent cultivating relationships is equally important. Friendships and loving family relationships take effort. Woody Allen once said, "90 percent of life, is showing up," and this is true for relationships too. Just showing up can go a long way, even when it requires more effort than we want to give.

When I was in second grade, I attended St. Anne's Catholic Grammar School. Those nuns were not nice to me, and yet my mother would always side with them no matter what they did. It was part of her Catholic upbringing, I suppose. There was the time I got smacked on the back of the head by St. Antonio Marie because she noticed the answers to my math problems were correct. The problem, according to her, was that I was not smart enough to get them right so she concluded that I must be cheating. When I came home and told my mother she looked at me and said, "Nancy, you should know the nuns are always right."

Thank God I managed to convince my parents to allow me to transfer to Stratford Avenue School, which was a public school. It was my very good luck to start my public school career with Mrs. Harrower. It was great not to have to curtsey every five minutes and eat in a cafeteria that smelled of tuna fish every Friday. Mrs. Harrower was an older woman in her late sixties. She wore dark red lipstick and she had short gray hair. Her knuckles were swollen with arthritis but she always had on red nail polish. She had been teaching for over 40 years and was strict but in a warm grandmotherly way.

One September day I came home from my new school as excited as I could be because once again we were doing something unheard of in Catholic School. We were having "Back to School" night. Each of us made names tags for our parents out of green construction paper. We had cut them in the shape of maple leaves and I thought they were so beautiful. We also had a folder, which held all our classwork. It was a way to show off our achievements to our curious, loving, and interested parents. I remember how excited I was for my parents to see my accomplishments and to meet my beloved new teacher.

That night as my mother made dinner I started to tell my mother what to expect at the meeting that night. I followed my mother all over the kitchen like an anxious puppy. "You are going to love Mrs. Harrower, she is so nice."

She listened and then said, "but I'm not going to go to back to school night. Listen Nancy, I've had five children before you who have been through the third grade and I know exactly what third graders do."

I was mortified. I just knew I would be the only one in my class to have parents that didn't show up. They would never see the beautiful maple leaves I made. My teacher would then know for sure that my parents didn't care about me. Couldn't they just pretend for one night? Why, for the love of God, did Mrs. Harrower have to know how much they didn't care? I was mortified.

When my father arrived home he could see that I was very upset. He asked me what was the matter and I explained it to him. We all ate dinner, and by then I was resigned to my humiliation. Then suddenly, he got up from watching TV in the den, and put on his coat. I was excited because I thought he was going to Carvel for ice cream to cheer me up.

When I asked him where he was going he said, "I am going to your 'Back to School' night to meet your teacher." I couldn't believe it. My dad was a lawyer and the most social creature on the planet.

He wasn't a "Back to School Night" kind of guy. I knew Mrs. Harrower would love Dad.

It seemed like an eternity until he got home. I couldn't wait to hear how it all went, to find out if he liked Mrs. Harrower, and see if he had read my short stories. When he came home he fixed us both a bowl of ice cream and he filled me in on everything that happened that night. He told me he liked my teacher very much and that she thought I was smart and had a great imagination. He explained to me how Mrs. Harrower is a little concerned because my math skills were not that great, but that I had beautiful handwriting. I could have sat there with my dad and that ice cream forever. It was so delicious to get some undivided attention and to be talking about me. It was the first time I felt like one of my parents had any real interest in me, and had a sense of who I was as an individual not just one of the seven.

The next day I went to school and the first thing I noticed was a note my father had written me in pencil on the desk. It was against the rules so I thought it was especially great. The note just said: "Hello, Cici," which was his nickname for me. Later that day when she asked us to open our books I noticed my dad had written on the very page we were working on. It tickled me and touched me to tears. My father's personal notes were all over my schoolwork. The notes he left were short, but very funny. I bragged and showed everybody what he had done. I was so full of pride. Everyone was jealous because I had a dad who was so cool and funny, and everybody could clearly see how much he loved me. It was the greatest day I ever had in school.

That one event taught me a very valuable life lesson. It showed me how important a small act of kindness can be, and how important showing up really is. Later in my life as a single mother when I thought a choral concert was too boring to go to, or if I felt to tired to go to a ball game, I would remember that day. Never forgetting how important it was for a child to have a parent that showed up.

I took care of my father during his dying days, and I made sure he knew how that day affected me. He said: "That is so funny because I never remember going, and yet you never forgot I went." My children and I were the beneficiaries of the lesson my father taught me those many years ago.

So try affirming yourself, and be excited about what your life can be. Be watchful for what you say to yourself. Only when we love ourselves and have enough personal happiness and satisfaction, do we have enough strength to show up and be fully present for those we love. So it's very important to love yourself and your life.

EXERCISE #6

Sometimes it's easy to forget how important it is to be kind to yourself, and to be kind to others. This exercise gives you a chance to reflect on this idea, and to focus on that question we've been asking all along: who's better than me?

1) Write down your 10 strongest assets. They can be personal, professional, objective, or subjective. They should not be accomplishments but rather character-driven assets. Use adjectives like: punctual, responsible, funny, warm, understanding, empathetic, thoughtful, kind, or generous.

2) Write down a daily affirmation that reinforces what you believe to be true about yourself. Saying it out loud at least once every day is very important. It is the only way your subconscious mind can absorb it and believe it.

3) Name the times you made the effort to show up for the important people in your life. What benefit came from showing up?

4) Name some times that others took the effort to show up in your life. How did you feel?

5) Now name the times you were disappointed by the people who didn't show up for you. How did it make you feel?

"Be careful about reading health books, you may die of a misprint."
—Mark Twain

Chapter 7:

Healthy Begets Happy

We Varsity women not only have to adjust to some emotional changes, but some physical ones as well. We all know about the joys of menopause. They made a musical about it, but then again, they also made a musical about the Titanic. Let's hope that menopause has a happier ending.

This time has often been referred to as "the change of life." It makes sense because it really does change our life. We are freed from worrying about pregnancy, and no longer have to endure the monthly visit from "our friend." Remember when that was code for your period? It's hilarious to

tried were kegel balls, or as I call them vaginal marbles. I was supposed to take these metal balls, insert them in my vagina, and use my kegel muscles to hold them in to tighten my vaginal wall and help with the incontinence. Of course, it didn't. I had to accept my fate that I would wear pads for the rest of my life. I was only 46 and already I was getting into Depends. I kept it a secret and I didn't talk about it with anyone.

I went back to my gynecologist and told her that the marbles and rings were probably okay for some women, but I needed something more powerful for my industrial size problem. I wasn't leaving until she heard me and came up with a reasonable solution. She recommended that I see a gyno-urologist. Ladies, please remember that term: GYNO-UROLOGIST. Look it up because it is what so many of us need.

My first appointment the nurse ushered me into the examination room and gave me a quart of water to drink, told me to put on the stupid paper gown, and wait for the doctor. I had to pee like crazy, but

I couldn't because I had to wait for the doctor. The door opens and in walked Dr. Kildare. All I thought was, "why couldn't I get Dr. Gilespie?" The first thing he asked me was to put my legs in the stirrups and me cough. I knew with a full bladder what was going to happen if I coughed, and I thought I would die of embarrassment. I begged him, "can I just tell what will happen? Do you have to see it?"

He assured me he did indeed need to see it. So, I coughed, and I pced a beautiful full arch. It was just as awful as it sounds. He told me that he knew exactly what was wrong with me, and said he could fix it.

He said there were three major contributing factors that made my problem so severe. The first was that I was fair skinned and blonde. He told me fair skinned women of Irish or Swedish decent are more prone to having this problem. He also told me it is hereditary, and having two children in one year only exacerbated my particular problem. There was however, a surgical procedure he could perform that would fix it all. The only caveat was I would have to give up smoking. He didn't want me under sedation for five hours with weak lungs, and he didn't want me to cough so hard that I would rip my stitches. We set a date for two months from that day and I promised him I would give up smoking the next day.

The next day I quit smoking, and the day after that I called the doctor and made an emergency appointment. I told him he had to prescribe something for me or I wouldn't be able to have the operation because I would be in Rikers Island doing time for homicide. He gave me a prescription of Wellbutrin, which I called my "happy pills," and I bought the nicotine patch. That was January 6, 2003. I haven't had a cigarette in more than 10 years. The operation was a total success and 11 months later, on November 2, 2003, I completed the New York City Marathon, speed walking 26.2 miles with dry pants and breathing like a champion.

Fixing my incontinence and giving up smoking was the key to my future without my knowing it. I had no idea how much my confidence was compromised by my incontinence and the shame I felt over my smoking habit. To this day I can remember standing out in the rain, in the cold, smoking, and watching people walk pass me. I could physically feel their disdain for my weakness. I was an addict. Back when I read the personals in the paper (before Match.com), everyone was looking for non-smokers. Instead of quitting, I just gave up dating, but once I gave up smoking and was no longer depending on Depends, I was back in the game, baby.

My husband Jack is not only a non-smoker, but he has asthma. If I had been smoking he wouldn't have been attracted to me, and if I were still incontinent, I wouldn't have been confident enough to date him. For five years I was on the road with the comedy trio "Mama's Night Out." Smoking would have made this a disaster. Most hotels we stayed at on the road were non-smoking and we traveled a lot by plane and then by car. Getting out constantly to smoke would just have been a nightmare.

Every day I am grateful I found the power and wisdom to give up smoking. People are only ready to quit, when they are ready to quit. I tried several times before and I was resentful and jealous of all the other people that could smoke. One time I even thought: "What if I get hit by a car today. That means I gave would have gone through all this sacrifice for nothing." When you begin to justify like that, you are not ready to quit anything.

It is amazing how one thing can change everything. So for any of you ladies who have this problem, or any other that you're embarrassed about—no matter what it is— do anything you can to fix it. If you are incontinent talk to your doctor and try to find a solution. If you don't enjoy sex or if it's painful, find a doctor you are comfortable talking with.

We can serve as great examples to our friends, family, and children by taking great care of ourselves. That goes for treatment for a bad back, arthritis, bunions, or whatever else compromises your feeling great. When people see us living a greater quality of life, it might just inspire them to do the same.

EXERCISE #7

1) Write down a list of things that ail you. From bunions to indigestion, from a sore back to a sore throat. Then make a general doctors appointment to address them. When you go take the list with you so you don't forget anything.

2) Name several things that will make you feel better overall (i.e. yoga class, walking, drinking more water, cutting down on junk food). Next to each item on that list write down how you could easily complete each thing. Maybe you bring a water bottle work, or maybe you'll join a local gym like Curves or the YMCA. But give yourself specific ways to make yourself feel better.

3) Make some reasonable and attainable health goals for yourself, name the steps you need to take to achieve them. Find a buddy to help keep you accountable and motivated. Have fun and I hope you feel better and better.

"Between the optimist and
the pessimist, the difference is droll.
The optimist sees the doughnut;
the pessimist the hole!"
—Oscar Wilde

Chapter 8:

It's Not Gray. It's Called Platinum!

Here's some good news. How you see yourself is entirely up to you. You can imagine yourself as:

- Young
- Old
- Happy
- Unhappy

- Fat
- Slim
- Rich
- Poor

Each one of these attributes are assigned by your point of view. Whether you are aware of it or not, how you feel about yourself, and your life, is often a matter of who you are comparing yourself to. When some people want to feel slim they compare themselves to one of the contestants on *The Biggest Loser*, if they want to feel young, then they go to a meeting of AARP. But that only helps in the short-term. If you don't compare yourself to anyone, it's easier to love and accept yourself as you are.

Shortly after I turned 50 and got re-married my perception of my life changed. I read *The Secret*. The book didn't impress me, but what interested me were the basic tenets of "ask, believe, receive." I think the secret may have gotten out though because the book sold over 16 million copies and it was featured on *Oprah*. After I read it, I realized that I had received everything I asked for. I never thought of it like that before, perhaps because I never asked for anything really BIG. Never did I want to be a "star." I was just happy to perform on a stage. I never wanted a big house. I just wanted to be able to pay my mortgage.

When I was a single mother, I can remember waiting in line at the grocery store with a few dollars in my pocket. In those days I always had to ask for a subtotal after every few items. I cringed every time they gave me the total, and I had less than that in my pocket. It seemed to just highlight my lack of abundance. I would say to myself: "Please let me be rich enough so that I won't ever have to ask for a subtotal again." I'm far from rich today, but I don't have to ask for subtotals any more. I'm as rich as I ever wanted to be. To this day, I'm still always grateful when I go to the food store and I don't have to panic when they run my debit card. I got exactly what I asked for.

My co-op was the first apartment I lived in, and I have lived here for the last 32 years. My greatest wish was that I could one day have a fireplace. Two years ago I saw an advertisement for a beautiful electric fireplace complete with a lovely mantle. The day I had it delivered felt like a dream come true. I now have the fireplace I never thought I could have.

In the years when my kids were growing up I drove the worst cars. They were humiliating and ugly, but they got me where

I had to go. Only in my day dreams would I dare to wish for a brand new convertible. That was high thinking for someone driving a car Fred Flintstone wouldn't be caught dead driving. After I married my husband it was time to turn in his leased truck, so we decided to get a brand new convertible. Another dream come true!

Once I saw things like this, I felt more powerful, as if I was able somehow to will it toward me. I felt more successful and more grateful. Yet nothing changed except my viewpoint, about the things I already had, or the things that had already happened. The events themselves remain the same. It is how we choose—and it is a choice—to see them that will decide how you experience your life. It doesn't take more effort to be positive than negative, but it does take more imagination.

My father hated telling bad news and he avoided it at all costs. He not only justified tragedy, but practically celebrated it. He could take anything tragic or sad, and put a positive spin on it. I was taught by a master how to "turn that frown upside down." He embraced a way of seeing events from the most optimistic viewpoint. He knew how to minimize troubles, and maximize joy. He was a genius at it. This technique has helped me get through many challenges in my life, and now as I am getting older I am happy to have it. Just for the record, I don't endorse completely how he did it, but I did learn a lot from it. Here are some examples of this art form:

1) In 1980 I was a newlywed in San Antonio, Texas. My grandmother lived in New York. We weren't particularly close, but she was elderly and I asked about her often. I moved back to New York to secure our new apartment, while Jimmy finished his stint in the air force. One night, while having dinner with my dad, I asked how Grandma was doing. He looked at me and without skipping a beat said, "Oh, I meant to tell you that she died." I almost

choked to death on a string bean. He didn't flinch he just said, "You weren't going to come all that way home for her funeral, and why would I upset you when you were so far away?" Uh…okay!

2) A few years ago my stepbrother Tommy was almost killed when he fell off of a five-story fire escape trying to get in the window of his locked apartment. I heard about it through the grapevine in town, because my father never called anyone with bad news. So, I stopped by his house and asked my father how Tommy was doing and my father said: "He's doing great. He's fantastic."

Later that day, I ran into Jean Gallic, a high school friend who happened to be Tommy's nurse in the hospital. I asked her when he was released from the hospital. She was shocked. "Nancy," she said, "right now he looks like that cartoon character Wily Coyote. He is in a total body cast from his head to his toes. He is traction and he broke every bone in his body. He'll be in the hospital for weeks, and rehab for months."

Of course, I went flying back to father's house, and screamed "What is wrong with you? How could you possibly tell me Tommy was great when he is in a total body cast? He will be in the hospital for weeks, and you made it sound like he could run the New York City marathon next week!"

My father stood up and got right in my face. He said in his strong booming voice, "Now you listen to me. I know poor Tommy has a few broken bones, but they'll heal, and he'll be fine. Today, by all rights, we should have been at Tommy O'Connor's funeral. So compared to dead, I think he's doing great. Fantastic." See how he spun that?

3) When my mother died, that was a harder spin for my Dad. She died on December 5, 1972, which was exactly eight days before my 16th birthday, and three weeks before Christmas. My father decided that out of respect for my mother we wouldn't send out Christmas cards that year. He also decided that we should instead, have our "First Annual McDougal Christmas Eve Party." He invited all the neighbors and all our friends, about 200 people in all. The tree was up, the lights were lit, the booze was flowing, and the house was filled with laughter, just as if no one important had died. The front door opens, and suddenly it looked like a scene out of Miracle on 34th Street. My Aunt Rose and Uncle Jerry came in with huge bags filled to the brim with presents.

As the night wore on we were all summoned into the living room. My sister Carol's boyfriend Dan Cashman started to make a speech. He told Carol he loved her and then asked her to look on a branch of the tree. What did she find? An engagement ring, which had been my mother's and had been on her own finger just three weeks before. So now champagne was flowing, people were crying and kissing, and we all were singing.

I was walking through the crowded merry house and passed one of the neighbors and I heard him say to his wife: "Didn't the mother just die?" The next day I told my father what I heard the neighbor say, and he said "We needed Christmas more this year than any other year. We all lost so much, and we needed to have some fun and some laughs, and to find something to celebrate. Your mother would have been so happy to see us all enjoying ourselves after so much sadness." From my father I learned that no matter the circum-

stances there is always something to
be grateful for.

One Christmas I took a page out of his
book. I had just started working for E.F.
Hutton in October, and they were supposed
to withhold the first two weeks pay but they
had inadvertently neglected to do it. They
found their error and rectified it in last
paycheck of the year, which I had already
decided I would use to buy the kids their
Christmas presents. I owed the phone company and the electric company, but I had
to be Santa Claus to my three- and four-
year-old. When I opened my check, I saw
it was for $67 and had a full blown nervous
breakdown. Thank God I worked with such
wonderful people. My co-worker Maxine
comforted me and told me she had a lot of
Barbie dolls and accessories she could buff
up and give to me. Her daughter was 13
and had outgrown them; they were in A+
condition. Tracy was another angel. She
assured me everything would fine, and en-

couraged me not to worry.

All day, I used every brain cell I possessed to come up with a plan to save Christmas. What did kids really love? What did they constantly want? Suddenly a light bulb lit over my head. I had a plan!

When I picked up the kids from daycare later that day, I used everything I learned from the American Academy of Dramatic Arts. I turned to them in the back seat and with the enthusiasm of a seven-year-old: "Guess who I talked to today." Without waiting for them to answer I said, "Santa Claus." They lost their minds, and bombarded with me with a million questions: "What did he say? Am I getting the Ninja Turtles? Did he get my letter? Does he know our names?"

I cut them off. "He told me this year he is going to do something just for you guys. This year he said you can have whatever you want. For breakfast. I don't mean pancakes or eggs, he said you can have anything! If you want brownies, you can have brownies. You want ice cream, you can have ice cream."

They were skeptical at first, but then Michael said tentatively, "could I have pizza?"

"Absolutely!"

The launch sequence was activated, in the middle of the night they woke me up. "Can we have pizza with bacon and a milkshake and brownies with ice cream over the brownies and M&Ms on top?"

I said, "Santa said you can have whatever you want, but you have to make up your mind because he has to go food shopping."

They got their list together and the next day was Christmas Eve. I took the kids to work because Santa was visiting the office, and we had a half day. Annie and Michael happily sat on Santa's lap. He gave Annie a beautiful Christmas dress from Lord & Taylor, and Michael got his Ninja Turtles.

Out of view of the children, my co-workers gave me a bag full of presents from everybody in the office. The mailroom chipped in and gave me an easel with a chalkboard and dry marker board; Maxine came through and had the Barbies wrapped in very festive mylar bags she got from the liquor store. Thank God Annie was too young to know about packaging. My boss, Scott Boylan, gave me a personal check for $100 dollars and I felt like the richest girl in town.

This happened 26 years ago. and it was the best most memorable, magical, Christmas of my life. I went home, put all the presents under the tree, and then I wrapped everything. I wrapped one glove, and the other one separately. Gum was placed in a shoebox with lots of tissue paper. Crayons were wrapped in a huge gift box, and a coloring book in a discarded Lord & Taylor box. The one thing I knew for sure, was at Christmas quantity is always better than quality. They would be just as happy to open a Game Boy as they would to open a book of stickers. Kids are idiots and I was smart enough to know it, and smarter still to take advantage of it. Don't get me wrong. I love my kids. They're like family!

That Christmas Eve night while the kids were sleeping, I wrapped all the presents and then tried to put the easel together. It was 4:30 AM, and no matter how hard I tried I could not get that easel together. I was frustrated, sad, anxious and exhausted. It was my first Christmas alone and I felt like a total failure. I put the TV on and *It's A Wonderful Life* was on every channel. I had never seen the very beginning, and I listened as it opens with the voice of God talking to Clarence, itching for his angel wings. God tells him to go to earth to help George Bailey. Clarence asks if he's sick, and God says, "no, it's much worse, he's discouraged."

All my angst, worry, and frustration bubbled up and I thought, "that's me." I was so discouraged, and I cried and cried and cried. When I was done I wiped my tears and approached my enemy: the easel. As I looked at it I realized I was trying to attach it upside down. Once I righted it, it was put together in no time. In that moment I realized I wasn't a hopeless loser and an incompetent Santa Claus. I was just discouraged and tired. I remembered what my mother told me many years ago: "nothing looks good when you're tired," so I put myself to bed.

The kids woke me in the morning and raced through opening their gifts and couldn't wait to have their breakfast. They giggled and laughed, and they felt like Santa's favorite kids because no one they knew had a Christmas breakfast like this. This became our traditional Christmas breakfast until the first year Jack and I shared as an engaged couple. That year I made eggs benedict. The kids were in their twenties and had been out on Christmas Eve celebrating. They were cranky when I woke them for the eggs.

"What is this yellow sauce?" my Mike asked.

"It's hollandaise sauce," I told him.

He looked at me and said, "I don't think I like it."

I screamed, "Oh, yes you do like it, and you are going to eat every bit of it!"

That was the last year we did that. We are back to old tradition of ice cream and brownies, and I still have my "magic hot chocolate" or what others might call Irish coffee. It works for us, it makes us happy, and it is our special tradition.

I have always been grateful that my father taught me the gift of optimistic thinking. It has served me, and my family well. I still use it today. There isn't anything I can't justify or wrap my head around. It reminds me of the quote by Albert Einstein "There are two ways to live: you can live as if nothing is a miracle; or you can live as if everything is a miracle." I prefer the latter.

So when we find ourselves getting older, and when life becomes more challenging find the most optimistic point of view, and see it from there. When people say to me, "your hair is the most beautiful 50 shades of gray," I tell them:

"It's not gray. It's called *platinum!*"

EXERCISE #8

How you look at your life has almost everything to do with your point of view. This exercise is designed to help you learn to spin positives out of negatives, and to adjust the way you see yourself. Having a positive outlook can change everything. Years ago if my car needed repairs I would have a nervous breakdown because I could never afford them. These days things are better for me financially, and though I don't like paying for them, I'm happy because at least I can pay for them. Now think of what's going on in your life and try to find ways to make things more positive.

1) Think back in your life and see what things you have asked for and received. It may be something that turned out well, or you may regret that you got it, but name it just the same.

EXERCISE #8 (con't)

2) Name an event you were unhappy about initially but were able to turn it around by seeing it in the most positive way.

3) What circumstance are you in now that you'd like to feel more positive about? Write it down, and then write the most positive spin you can think of as a way of dealing with it.

4) Write 10 of the most positive things in your life right now.

5) Write 10 negative things in your life right now, and then rewrite them with a more positive way to see them. Not every negative can be turned positive easily, but at the very least we can learn from every bad thing that happens to us and apply that learning towards future situations.

"An archeologist is the best husband any woman can have. The older she gets, the more interested he is in her."
—Agatha Christie

Chapter 9:

The Best Is Yet to Come

My entire life I've been hopeful that things will get better. However, even I, the cockeyed optimist, never thought my life would be more fun over 50 than it was under 30. I'm not the only one either. More women celebrating their 60th birthdays tell me the same thing. So I want you to know it's true, the best is yet to come. Single women over 50 tell me all the time how they would like to meet men, but that men their age are only interested in younger women. The truth is that any man over 60 who would date a woman in her thirties is not the kind of man you would want to date anyway. The punishment for him is that he thinks dating someone younger will make him feel younger, but it won't. It will only make him feel older.

There was the old joke about a woman of 30 married to a man of 75. She suspects he is cheating on her so she hires a private detective. Sure enough she finds that every Wednesday he meets the same woman at the local hotel in room 303. So one Wednesday she goes to the hotel and knocks on the door and catches them together. She is shocked to see that the woman he is with is 70-years-old. She screams at her husband and says: "Why would you cheat on me with a woman like this, what could she possibly have that I don't have." He just looked at her and said, "patience."

The trick to finding someone after 50 is to be motivated, know what you are looking for, and believe you can get it. This is where all your life skills come into play. You need to be confident, and courageous, and you need to feel sexy and strong. Let me be very clear, it's not what other people think, or what you look like. It is what you believe about yourself that will determine how you feel, which will determine everything. If you think you are sexy you will appear sexy no matter your age or what you look like. Remember *The Golden Girls*—those women went on dates every week with older men, and it was all because they were strong women who were confident in who they were. That may have been a fictional television show, but we could still learn a thing or two from those women.

If you'd like to date, you have to get into the dating arena, which means you have to get out of your house and into the world, hopefully in a place where there are men. The best way to meet people is to go to places and be with people that are like-minded. If you like to bowl join a bowling league. If you like to hike join a club for hikers. Just don't join if you don't like bowling or hiking because the person you meet will then want to do it every weekend, and you'll have to go.

The best place to meet people is

through friends. You could meet someone at a party, a wedding, or a barbecue. You never know when someone will bring a brother, co-worker, or divorced friend along. For sure you're not meeting anyone sitting by yourself in your living room, unless of course you're Skype dating. But even then, eventually you have to go out and go on an actual date. Things you want don't just magically appear in your life. You have to make them happen. The best way to a happy future is to create it yourself.

This is an interesting time to be single. More people are getting divorced after 50 than at any other time in history. There are plenty of available men out there—you just need to find them. So enter the dating world with the powerful combination of optimism and confidence.

Being a stage comedian is a bit like going on a date—it's just a date with an entire room of people. Audiences will pick up on nonverbal cues almost immediately. If the person on stage is nervous and jittery, it makes the audience uncomfortable, and it's the same feeling being on a date with someone who is insecure. We all know what a terrible feeling that is, when the person we are with wants something from us that we're not sure we want to give them. People like being with people who are complete. We feel safe in the company of someone who is self-assured.

If you'd like to meet someone, then you better know the kind of person you'd like to find. It's just like shopping for a dress for a big event. When you find the one, you say, "ahhhh, just what I was looking for." This is not the time in your life to settle for second best. No marriage or relationship is better than a bad one. It is the time in our life when we should know ourselves well enough that we won't get stuck with someone who isn't for us. But keep your mind open because you never know what your soul mate will be disguised as.

By the time I met my husband I was ready. I had spent the previous 10 years doing comedy every weekend with my old friends and meeting new ones all the time.

It was my career and it doubled as my social life. There was no need for Match.com because I had all the love and attention I wanted from the people who also made me laugh and made me feel like a star. Comedy was my shield against the real world where people weren't always as kind, and where I felt less confident. On stage I felt safe, strong, and powerful. Out in the world, I felt a little less worthy.

After the show on Saturday nights we would all go out and have a ball. When the hour grew late, some of the guys were going out later and looking for a hook-up. There was nothing for me at any of the places they were going to, so I would head home alone. Then, one night as I was going home on the train alone, as I always did, I knew I wanted more. All at once I felt lonely and left out and I realized I wanted someone to come home to. My father used to say, "everyone needs someone to 'gunk' around with!" For years there had been an entire gaggle of wonderful, fun, entertaining friends, but now I wanted a more intimate relationship, something meaningful, I wanted love.

So I joined Weight Watchers and created a profile on Match.com. It was very scary. In your profile they ask you to describe yourself. It was very hard because beauty and personality are so subjective. I thought, do I downplay myself so I don't disappoint anyone?

"I have been told my best qualities are that I have wonderful posture and good hearing. The New York blood bank told me I have great platelets."

But I was afraid that if I wrote something strong like, "I'm a funny, outgoing, woman with a knack for having fun," that I would open the door and say, "Hi," and my date would say, "I thought you said you were funny. 'Hi' isn't funny."

I really wanted to meet someone, so I went ahead and posted the requisite photo and profile. And for a few weeks, I winked and poked at people, and they winked and poked at me back. A few dates were secured. None were awful, but none were great either. So I quit, but I had dipped my big toe in the dating pool. That was powerful enough. When I went out, I found myself being more open to men and acting in a more flirtatious way. I was also paying more attention to my looks. Joining Weight Watchers and losing 15 pounds was my way of making myself feel better, more attractive, and in control of my life. The truth is, the weight I lost wasn't enough to make a difference to the outside world, but it served to make me feel more confident in the terrifying dating arena. By the time that fateful night arrived, I was prepared for it. I had been looking for him. He just had to show up, and he did.

I met my husband when I was 49-years-old. My good friend Tommy had just buried his mother, and after the funeral we went back to his house in Point Lookout, New York. It is a tiny seaside town wedged between the bay and the Atlantic Ocean. It was January 27, 2006, and after being at Tommy's house the group of us decided to go out in town. There was only one bar open. It was called the Bay House. It was the local dive, but behind the taps was a beloved local bartender named Jack Bella. In all my years of going out in Point Lookout and even though we had several mutual friends, our paths had never crossed.

I walked into the Bay House (and after several drinks at Tommy's), took one look at Jack leaned over the bar and said: "You are adorable." The magic of alcohol! He looked at me and said, "and what are you drinking young lady?" I never order this drink, and I don't know what compelled me to order it that night, but I said, "I would like a Bloody Mary."

Behind the bar there are no lemons, no celery sticks, and there is no tomato juice. He cracked open a Coors Light, slammed it down on the bar with a huge smile, and said: "There's your Bloody Mary. The next bar is eight miles away. Welcome to the Bay House."

To me, it was absolutely the funniest thing I ever heard a bartender say. I began to flirt shamelessly with Mr. Jack. Between the weight I had lost, and the alcohol I had consumed, I was now in this overly confident delusional state . I thought I was totally hot. We flirted and laughed, and at one point I gave him the nod signaling for the two of us to meet in the kitchen. We made out like teenagers.

Our friends figured this out as the bartender went missing and so did their inebriated friend, and they thought it was hilarious. When they asked Jack what I was doing with him in the kitchen, he said, without missing a beat, "she was helping me do inventory."

The next day I had a terrible hangover. I had gotten an email from Jack and a phone call as well. I asked Tommy if we could go back to the Bay House that night. I knew Jack was working, but to be honest I didn't really remember exactly what he looked like and I wanted to make sure he was a good guy before I agreed to a date. So we went back to the Bay House. We had a beer at the bar. The door opened and in walked Jack. During my single years I use to try to envision what my ideal man would like. I used try to pick out which actors I thought would be my type. As hard as I tried over the years I could never picture him. They were too Irish, or too Italian, too old or too young. Eventually I gave up trying to picture Mr. Wonderful. Then the door to the Bay House opened and there was the face. I knew it immediately. It seemed as if I was waiting for that face my whole life. He looked at me with his beautiful smile and wonderful sense of humor, and said, "Hello, Shveetie!" We talked that night and I left knowing we had a future.

For my birthday that year, Tommy and his wife Lisa had given me an airline ticket and hotel room in Tortola in the British Virgin Islands. Our other dear friend Donna Snyder was coming as well. All the people in Point Lookout took their winter vacations there. We all tried to convince Jack he should come too. The Bay House was going to be closed the week we were going. He said he thought it was too expensive especially because it was so last minute. We were leaving on February 13th, and it was already February 4th.

Jack and I had known each other only three weeks, but we were never able to go on a date. There were blizzards, and I had shows, and we just never got together. He told me he wanted to see me before I left to go to Tortola. Since we were booked on a very early flight on a Tuesday morning, I was staying at Tommy and Lisa's place on Monday night. I finally was able to spend more time with Jack (along with eight other friends). We had a lot of laughs talked all through the night. Finally at around 6:00 AM, I had to throw him out. As we kissed good night on the front stoop he looked at me and said, "I'm going to try to make it down to Tortola. If I can't make there I'll at least pick you up at the airport when you get back." The problem was that Tommy had made all the arrangements, so I couldn't give him any information. I didn't know myself where I was staying. We did have a mutual friend who was coming back from exactly where I was going. I said to Jack, "if you decide you want to come, just ask

Don Sweeney, he'll know where it is."

We arrived in Tortola on Valentine's Day. The place was tropical, beautiful, casual, and fun. There was a great tiki hut with a Jimmy Buffet cover band and the tropical drinks were flowing. The three of us had dinner that night, and I said, "I'm sure Jack Bella will never make it here, but if he does I will marry him, because between the plane, the boats, and automobiles, getting here is like climbing Mount Everest."

The next day we were on the beach and having a grand old time, meeting people, and making plans to meet at happy hour. I went to my room took a shower, got myself made up and dressed and headed to happy hour to listen to Jimmy Buffet songs and drink my favorite rum drinks. As I opened the door there was a little post it stuck to the door and written on it was: "Jack Bella called he'll be on the 2:30 ferry tomorrow please call him." I was never so shocked in my life! I ran—and I mean ran—to Tommy's and Lisa's cottage. They were absolutely shocked.

I always say that our first date was six days in Tortola. What a way to get to know each other. From that moment on we knew we were the real deal. Jack had been married for 30 years and had been divorced about five years when we met. I had been married for five years and divorced for 20. We knew we were great together, and there had been so much missing in our lives for so long. We just knew we wanted to be married.

At the time we had been dating for about six months, and at our respective ages, 49 and 59, and we were certainly a committed couple deeply in love. Knowing how rare it is to find such a good man, especially at my age, my goal was to keep him alive. Jack needed a physical, and I said I would go with him. I got a referral of a wonderful doctor and we made a double appointment at 1PM on July 25, 2006. When we arrived, the receptionist handed him clipboard with forms to be filled out. The questionnaire asked the name of the person who he would allow access to his medical records. Under name, he wrote: "Nancy Witter." Next to my name it asked what my relationship to him was.

He snapped his head like a light bulb had gone on, then put pen back to paper and finished filling out the form. When he was done he handed me the clipboard and said, "Do me a favor and just look at this to see if I filled it out right."

I took the clipboard and was poised with a pen in my hand ready to correct any mistakes he may have made. Next to my name where it said, "relationship" he had written what he thought was "fiancé" with a question mark next to it. I looked at it, and then I looked back up at him. There he was staring at me with a huge smile stretched across his face, with his eyebrows raised like a facial question mark.

At first I couldn't believe what I was reading, and that he was asking me to marry him in the waiting room of a doctor's office. My immediate reaction was an overwhelming sense of absolute love, and total joy. I looked at the paper again, and then looked up into the eyes of my future husband. Then I said to him, with a lump in my throat and a smile on my face as I handed him back the clipboard: "I know what you mean, but you wrote finance."

We were married exactly one year from our first date in Tortola. My son Michael walked me down the aisle, and my daughter Annie was my maid of honor. Jack's son Brendan was his best man, and his daughter Devon escorted her dad down the aisle. The rest of the guest list was 30 of our closest friends. Not many people share their honeymoon with 30 friends, but it worked perfect for us! My gay friends were the best bridesmaids I could have asked for. They made Jack look like a million bucks and helped me into my Spanx, which is by the way, just a really nice name for girdle! They all hummed, "Here Comes The Bride" as I walked onto the beach. We ate, drank, lounged in the sun, played in the water, sang, snorkeled, toured the island. It was the time of my life and when I least expected it.

The Best Is Yet to Come

I never expected to find love again and marry at 50. I hope this story serves as hope for any woman out there feeling the same way. There are a lot of ways to meet people, and if that doesn't work out—there are also a lot of bartenders. Just stay away from mine because he's already taken!

EXERCISE #9

This exercise is meant to help you find your bliss. What are you hoping for right now? It can be difficult to try to find love at any age, but you just need to remember: who's better than me? Who wouldn't want to be with me? Use these questions to help get the ball rolling.

1) Name at least three different and specific ways you could meet someone. (i.e., dating websites, friends, activities)

2) What are your non-negotiables? (i.e., non-drinker, not married)

3) What are the qualities that are the most important to you? (i.e. intelligent, sense of humor, kind)

4) What are you most confident about?

5) What are you most proud of?

6) What would make you your happiest? (i.e. love, job, new career, new home)

7) Name your best qualities that you bring to a relationship.

Now that you've written this down, let's come up with an action plan. You know who you are, but now what do you have to do to get you from dreaming to scheming? An action plan should consist of a series of steps that lead you towards your goal. What I'm talking about is finding ways to boost your confidence and make yourself open and available.

"The greater danger for most of us lies not in setting our aim too high and falling short; but in setting our aim too low, and achieving our mark."
—Michelangelo

Chapter 10:

Good Luck and God Bless!

After writing down my stories, turning my gray to platinum, and looking myself in the mirror with affirmations, I was able to do amazing things. I became a successful comedian. I quit smoking. I found the love of my life. And you know why? It's because I was able to ask myself a simple question. Who's better than me? You can have everything that you want too, because, well, who's better than you?

It was hard to transition from working in a bank and performing comedy to becoming a life coach and writer. I find I've morphed into an entrepreneur, but without the perfect skill set for that kind of work. It is a challenge. It has been difficult, rewarding, scary, and fun. I have been stuck and unstuck, I have failed and succeeded, bombed on stage and killed, so when I speak about these issues they are coming from firsthand knowledge.

What I wanted from this book was to encourage women of all ages, but especially to those that are transitioning into the middle years—from marriage to divorce, from working to retirement, from downsizing to the empty nestering. Change is hard. Life can be overwhelming and we need all the help we can get. I wanted to remind women that this is your life, and it's important. It's always worth the effort.

So whether you need to work less, sleep more, change jobs, ask for help, or whatever, do it. Value how important you are, and how important your happiness is. You will be better to those you love when you are doing what is best for you. To help, I have made a list of things that will make you feel more positive in a negative world. I've also got some exercises and tips for getting your life in order and to help you to keep moving forward.

Kindness: Maya Angelou said: "I've learned that people will forget what you said, people will forget what you did, but people will never forget how you made them feel." Try random (or not so random) acts of kindness whenever you can. When you make someone feel better about themselves, it can't help but make you feel better about yourself. Please know how powerful you and your words and your deeds are. They can change a person's day, week, or even her life.

Turn off the TV: Once in a while, we have to turn off the news. Don't believe everything you hear. I read that we have endorphins and serotonin coursing through our veins, and if we didn't life would scare us to death. So when the news begins to overwhelm you, step away. Life is scary enough. Take a walk outside, start a creative project, and most of all, just do something that makes you feel good. Get that serotonin pumping.

Friendships: My mother always said: "Show me your friends and I will show you who you are." Cultivate, and cherish your friendships. They define who we are. They are the "gloom-chasers" of our lives. Take care of your friends, and make sure to keep your connections alive. And I mean in person—not just over Facebook or e-mails once every six months.

Sleep: Get enough sleep. It is how we heal. How much we get or don't get affects our bodies in ways that could be terrible. One of the best methods to improve your sleep is to remove the televisions, computer, and workout equipment. Give yourself fewer distractions and just focus on winding down for a peaceful rest every night. You deserve it.

Eat: When necessary eat chocolate and ice cream. Okay, so, I know I should be telling you to try health foods, and that fruits and vegetables will make you feel fresh. But let's be honest: there is nothing that will make you feel better faster than a grilled cheese sandwich and cup of tomato soup.

Read: Find a great book that moves and inspires you. The things we spend our time on become who we are, whether we're talking about friends, television, books, or whatever. The better stuff you spend time with, the better you become. I have listed some recommended reading at the end of this chapter, but read what makes you happy, and what inspires you to go out do something. If a trashy romance novel is what you love, and it encourages you to be more open in your relationships, then go for it. If you think a self-help book will help you to get over a hurdle in your life, then read it. Just try to consume as much infor-mation that will help you to be the person you want to be.

Watch: Go see a funny movie with a great friend, or attend a play, concert, comedy show, opera, or even a circus. Just find something, anything, that lifts and amazes you. Make a day of it, and make a habit of it. Live entertainment will always lift your spirits.

Generosity: Be generous with your time, your love, and your money. Remember you have what someone else needs. It may be your friendship, your counsel, or just your company. When we give our personal gifts, we receive the most. If you feel helpless, help someone.

Show up: I can't say this enough. Simply showing up is one of the most important things we can do. Show up for your friends, your kids, your family, and for yourself. Your presence is always a present.

Forgive: Forgive a foe, and most of all forgive yourself. Give everybody the benefit of the doubt. Assume the best before you believe the worst. It will lift a burden and will make your life lighter.

Good Luck and God Bless!

Gratitude: Do you remember Bing Crosby's advice that he sang from White Christmas? He sang: "When I'm worried and I can't sleep, I count my blessings instead of sheep; and I fall asleep counting my blessings. When my bankroll is getting small, I think of when I had none at all, and I fall asleep counting my blessings." I am grateful for all things—my health, friends, family, great wine, a great meal, good laughs, and most of all for love. You probably have all of these things in your life too, and you probably have more to be thankful for. Whether it's something as small as getting a good parking spot, or as big like a near-miss car accident, just be grateful for everything that's good in your life. Feeling thankful for every day is not a bad way to go to sleep each night.

Love: Be cognizant of it every day. Be grateful for it, surround yourself as often as you can with the people you love, and make sure they know you love them.

Believe: Remember the New York Mets' slogan in 1969: "You Gotta Believe!" Nobody thought they could win the World Series, but they did because they believed. And you have to too. Believe in possibilities and impossibilities. Believe in yourself and your potential. Believe in your kids and your families. Remember Captain "Sully" Sullenberger who landed Flight 1549 on the Hudson River. Impossible things happen every day, but only if you believe that they can.

Celebrate: Life is too short not to appreciate and enjoy the victories and the milestones whenever they appear. So celebrate birthdays, New Year's, anniversary, promotions at work, weight loss, getting a great deal on shoes, and anything else you can think of. It is a way of showing gratitude for your good fortune. It's also a way to bring friends and family together for a positive reason. Raise your glass, and eat some cake, because we can never underestimate how important it is to share our victories with the ones we love.

Be a Kid: Go to the zoo, go to an amusement park, or a museum just for the fun of it. Bring a child with you or go by yourself. It is a way of being awed again by looking at a giraffe or riding a roller coaster. It will remind you the world is still an awesome place.

Dream: Write down all your hopes and dreams. Cut out pictures from magazines or from the Internet. You can paste them into your notebook, or you can create a dream board. Is it a house by the ocean you're dreaming of, or a cute boyfriend, a new car, a better job? Creating visual representations of your dreams is a way of keeping your hopes alive and in front of you. It's fun to dream, and the more real you can make it, the more fun it is.

Exercises for a Better Life

At the end of each chapter I have tried to share exercise that I hope you will find helpful. Here are a few more to keep you motivated toward finding your better life, and accomplishing everything you want and need.

1) List Your Greatest Annoyances:

One day the light went out in my refrigerator. Every time I went to the store I meant to pick up a light bulb, but I kept forgetting. For three months I went without a light in my refrigerator, and I felt like Helen Keller every time I tried to reach for the ketchup. Finally I got the bulb, put it in and it was as if I hear God saying, "let there be light."

I always like to say: "When you lose, don't lose the lesson." Not having a light in my refrigerator was a small annoyance compared to the other things I've been through, but these small things get in the way of our lives. It was so easy to fix, and yet it made my life miserable for so long.

All of these life annoyances are small but powerful because they can drain us of our precious energy. How often do you grab your coat in the morning, only to have a Dick Van Dyke moment where everything practically falls on top of you? "One of these days I have to clean that closet," you say. But each time that happens, it gets stored in your brain as a burden. Many of us have several of these types of annoyances before we leave the house. The button on our coat is missing, the car door handle needs to fixed, or the kids need new shoes again. All those things bother you and zap your energy.

So I want you to write a list of at least 50 things, large and small, that annoy you the most. I know you can come up with at least that many, and hopefully not too many more. After you've written them down put the list somewhere where you will see it every day. As you start to fix the things on the list scratch them off. It will give you a wonderful sense of achievement. They can be as small as changing a light bulb to as large as selling your house. The idea is that you are taking personal inventory of those things in your physical life that have become a silent burden. The more we tolerate these annoying things the more we tolerate other things in other areas of our life. To really examine what is going on in your life and attempt to make it better is a way to honor yourself and the quality of your life. So get that list and write it all: Big and small.

2) Mind Dump:

I've seen a different version of this in Julia Cameron's *The Artist's Way* she calls them "Morning Notes," but in my version, I always called it my "mind dump." It is a way of getting everything out of head and onto the page every morning. The idea is get rid of all the random thoughts we have in our heads that get in the way of our good intentions for the day. It's not a to-do list, as much as it's a way to get rid of negative thoughts as we lead into the day. I use it just to see what shows up on the page and sometimes I'm shocked. As you all know by now, I'm a big believer in writing as therapy, to see things more clearly, to keep track of your life, and to see what shows up. It also gives you a little me time. It is a great habit and one I really recommend. Once you finish your mind dump, you're ready to have a wonderful and productive day.

3) Goal Tracking:

I find it helpful to do this exercise every week. On Sunday write down "The Week in Review" in your notebook. Recount all of the minor and major successes you had during the past week, your challenges, and what you learned. Then write your goals for the upcoming week.

The following Sunday review your goals to see which you achieved and which you didn't. Review the goals you didn't accomplish and try to figure out what held you back. Maybe it wasn't really important to you and you can remove it from the list. Maybe you just didn't have time, so you can move it to the top of your list for the following week. But if there's some other reason or some other thing that held you back from completing your goals, it's important to get to the bottom of it.

Your accomplishment can be anything. Sometimes my goals are to watch less TV that week, to make healthier food choices, or to go to the gym when I don't feel like it. You need to find ways to pat yourself on the back, and to give yourself challenges for the week to come. The more focused you are on your life, the more likely it is to improve. You have to pay attention to your life. If you want to write about something that was not successful always remember to follow that up with what you learned from it.

4) Mental Health Days

Sometimes in our busy world it is a real joy to give yourself a mental health day. It might mean calling in sick to work and staying home to do nothing. Go to the movies by yourself. Read a book you've been meaning to get to. Or if it gets you going, clean out the closet. When you find yourself overwhelmed, over-worked, under-appreciated, give yourself a break and do something for you.

Corporate America is terrible at giving employees the proper amount of time to rejuvenate. Stay-at-home moms or people with non-traditional careers should do the same. We all work hard without the proper amount of time to resuscitate ourselves. We all need a vacation sometimes, so we can find that disconnect. So put away your work cell phones, and don't check your e-mails. It's time to get a sitter, call in sick, and give yourself the gift of a mental health day!

Recommended Reading

Who's Better Than Me?

I love books that enrich our lives. I loved writing this book, and there have been many other writers that have inspired me on my journey. Here are some of my favorites that just lifted my spirits and gave me some really valuable insights:

Think and Grow Rich
by Napoleon Hill

How to Win Friends and Influence People
by Dale Carnegie

Awaken The Giant Within
by Anthony Robbins

Excuse Me, Your Life Is Waiting
by Lynn Grabhorn

The Power of Positive Thinking
by Dr. Norman Vincent Peale

Change Your Thoughts, Change Your Life
by Dr. Wayne Dyer

Chicken Soup for the Soul

Good Luck and God Bless!

by Jack Canfield and Mark Victor Hansen

These are just a few of thousands of great inspirational life affirming books you can read. We get what we focus on, and we become what we spend time with. That goes not only for the people we spend time with, but the things we read and the programs we watch. So be aware of how you are spending your time.

There is nothing in this book that I haven't experienced myself. I've gone through hard times and great times. I'm still trying new things. I hope I will succeed, and I know I might fail. To me it's worth the risk. I'm following my heart, and pursuing my passion. Please know if you have enough courage, confidence, humor, and belief in yourself, you can create the life you want and live happily ever after! When you do, and even when you just try, remember one thing. I want you to roll your eyes upward, grin and say out loud:

Who's better than me?

Good luck and God bless!

Acknowledgments

There were a lot of people who inspired, guided, and supported me during the process of writing this book. First, I'd like to thank my editor Tom Hardej for knowing exactly what my vision was, and for helping me manifest it. Your kind and candid guidance helped to make me a better author. You made my dream come true. You were just what I needed, when I needed it! Thank you, Tom.

I will be forever grateful to my lifelong friend, Carol Manire, for knowing my voice better than I know my own. Her unwavering support and guidance has been such a wonderful gift in my life. Everyone should be as lucky as I am to have such a wonderful friend. Thank you, thank you, thank you. Special thanks to Connor Manire too, for making my heart soar, and my face smile every Wednesday!

I'd also like to thank my sister Ditta Scully for for being such a loving supporter to me my whole life. Thanks for reading this book 100 times, and for being a great speller. You made me look smart! To my sisters Carol Cashman and Peanut Shupe, thanks for always believing I was better than I thought I was! As my mother would say "You're very lucky to have each other." I am also grateful and thankful to Jeanette Freda, Jane O'Keeffe, Cathy Carney, and Annie and Michael Witter for being such wonderful cheerleaders. Your love and encouragement has helped me become, what I always wanted to become. You're the stuff made in heaven!

Finally to my husband and favorite bartender Jack Bella. He is a little upset he doesn't appear until Chapter 9, but that's because in my life he didn't show up...until Chapter 9! Thank you for always believing in me, and for thinking I'm smarter than I am!

About the Author

Growing up in a very large Irish "Cathaholic" family gave Nancy Witter all the comedic material she would need to sustain her through her prolific comedy career. She has won four New York City MAC Awards for "Outstanding Female Comedy." She made her television debut on Nick at Nite's *Search for the Funniest Mom in America* as one of five finalists. For years she performed in theaters across the country in the smash hit comedy trio "Mama's Night Out." Nancy has appeared on television on *Mom's Cooking*, on *The Dr. Oz Show* in an Iron Chef competition, and on *Nick Mom Night Out*.

In 2007, Nancy fell in love and married Jack Bella. This life-changing event served to give her not only a new name, but also a new outlook on life. Toward that end she enrolled at NYU and received her Professional Certification in Life Coaching. Nancy is now combining her life coaching

and comedic skills as a professional motivational speaker. Her talks, like her book, are
a lighthearted and insightful look at aging,
change, courage and choices. Her goal is to
help women get re-inspired about their lives
and have a laugh all along the way!

Made in the USA
Middletown, DE
17 November 2019